W9-BLE-536

VOGUE KNITTING

TODDLER KNITS

VOGUE KNITTING

TODDLER KNITS

SOHO PUBLISHING COMPANY
NEW YORK

SOHO PUBLISHING COMPANY
233 Spring Street
New York, New York 10013

Library of Congress Cataloging-in-Publication Data

Vogue knitting toddler knits / [editor-in-chief, Trisha Malcolm]. -- 1st ed.
p. cm. – (Vogue knitting on the go!)
ISBN 1-931543-03-8
1. Knitting–Patterns. 2. Children's clothing I. Title: Toddler knits. II. Malcolm,
Trisha, 1960- III. Series.

TT825 .V6473 2001
747.43'20432–dc21   00-066767

Manufactured in China

1 3 5 7 9 10 8 6 4 2

First Edition

TABLE OF CONTENTS

INTRODUCTION

If you have a two to four-year-old in your life, you know how hard it is to keep up with toddlers—in more ways than one! These busy little people seem to grow as fast as they move; they demand clothes that wear well and have an insatiable appetite for bright colors and playful details. Fortunately for knitters, this addition to the Knitting on the Go series provides delightful designs that can be completed before these dynamic tykes explode right out of toddlerhood.

The projects featured in this book ensure that the cardigans, rompers, pullovers, and accessories within these pages can be completed for pint-sized toddlers in the "found moments" during a knitter's busy day. Necessary naps, play dates at the park, and even time-outs can provide enough time to work a few stripes or craft a flower appliqué. In some cases, bulky yarns and one-piece construction speed up the process; in others, the small sizes of the pieces allow for a little extra time spent on clever cables and bobbles, bright and boisterous colorwork, and fanciful embellishments.

Each piece in this book is designed to be as satisfying and fun for a knitter to knit as it will be for a toddler to wear. You won't want to waste any time in starting these charming pieces—and besides, no toddler is going to wait—so grab your needles and get a jump on and **KNIT ON THE GO!**

THE BASICS

Knitting a sweater or personal object for a small child is always a heartfelt production. By the time a child reaches the age of two, his or her own unique personality and particular taste begin to appear. When you knit a precious gift for a child of two, three, or four, you can help to meet that child's need to express—and dress—a budding personality.

We have gathered together 21 designs that reflect the special personalities of the designers who created them as well as the children who will wear them. With the appropriate materials, concise, easy-to-follow instructions, and an idea of your toddler's tastes, you're ready to create a beautiful design straight from the heart.

SIZING

Most of the garments in this book are written for sizes 2, 3, and 4, allowing extra ease for your child to grow into the garment. Some sleeves are knit from the top down; that is, the stitches are picked up along the underarm, and the sleeve width is decreased down to the cuff. This is an especially helpful technique for toddlers' sweaters because the sleeve length can be easily adjusted later on. Since children's measurements change so rapidly, it is best to measure your child or a sweater that fits well to determine which size to make.

YARN SELECTION

For an exact reproduction of the projects photographed, use the yarn listed in the "Materials" section of the pattern. We've chosen yarns that are readily available in the U.S. and Canada at the time of printing. The Resources list on pages 94 and 95 provides addresses of yarn distributors. Contact them for the name of a retailer in your area.

YARN SUBSTITUTION

You may wish to substitute yarns. Perhaps you view small-scale projects as a chance to incorporate leftovers from your yarn stash, or the yarn specified may not be available in your area. You'll need to knit to the given gauge to obtain the knitted measurements with a substitute yarn (see "Gauge" on page 11). Be sure to consider how the fiber content of the substitute yarn will affect the comfort and the ease of care of your projects.

To facilitate yarn substitution, *Vogue Knitting* grades yarn by the standard stitch gauge obtained in stockinette stitch. You'll find a grading number in the "Materials" section of the pattern, immediately following the fiber type of the yarn. Look for a substitute yarn that falls into the same category. The suggested needle size and gauge on the yarn

GAUGE

It is always important to knit a gauge swatch, and it is even more so with garments to ensure proper fit.

Patterns usually state gauge over a 4"/10cm span; however, it's beneficial to make a larger test swatch. This gives a more precise stitch gauge, a better idea of the appearance and drape of the knitted fabric, and a chance for you to familiarize yourself with the stitch pattern.

The type of needles used—straight or double-pointed, wood or metal—will influence gauge, so knit your swatch with the needles you plan to use for the project. Measure gauge as illustrated. Try different needle sizes until your sample measures the required number of stitches and rows. *To get fewer stitches to the inch/cm, use larger needles; to get more stitches to the inch/cm, use smaller needles.*

Knitting in the round may tighten the gauge, so if you measured the gauge on a flat swatch, take another gauge reading after you begin knitting. When the piece measures at least 2"/5cm, lay it flat and measure over the stitches in the center of the piece, as the side stitches may be distorted.

It's a good idea to keep your gauge swatch in order to test blocking and cleaning methods.

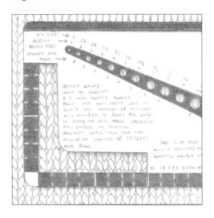

label should be comparable to that on the "Yarn Symbols" chart (see page 16).

After you've successfully gauge-swatched a substitute yarn, you'll need to figure out how much of the substitute yarn the project requires. First, find the total length of the original yarn in the pattern (multiply number of balls by yards/meters per ball). Divide this figure by the new yards/meters per ball (listed on the yarn label). Round up to the next whole number. The answer is the number of balls required.

FOLLOWING CHARTS

Charts are a convenient way to follow colorwork, lace, cable, and other stitch patterns at a glance. When knitting back and forth in rows, read charts from right to left on right side (RS) rows and from left to right on wrong side (WS) rows, repeating any stitch and row repeats as directed in the pattern. When knitting in the round, read charts from right to left on every round. Posting a self-adhesive note under your working row is an easy way to keep track of your place.

LACE

Lace knitting provides a feminine touch. Knitted lace is formed with "yarn overs," which create an eyelet hole in combination with decreases that create directional effects. To make a yarn over (yo), merely pass the yarn over the right-hand needle to form a new loop. Decreases are worked as k2tog, ssk, or SKP depending on the desired slant and are spelled out specifically with each instruction. On the row or round that follows the lace or eyelet detail, each yarn over is treated as one stitch. If you're new to lace knitting, it's a good idea to count the stitches at the end of each row or round. Making a gauge swatch in the stitch pattern enables you to practice the lace pattern. Instead of binding off the swatch, place the final row on a holder, as the bind off tends to pull in the stitches and distort the gauge.

COLORWORK KNITTING

Two main types of colorwork are explored in this book: intarsia and stranding.

Intarsia

Intarsia is accomplished with separate bobbins of individual colors. Use this method for large blocks of color. When changing colors, always pick up the new color and wrap it around the old color to prevent holes.

Stranding

When motifs are closely placed, colorwork is accomplished by stranding along two or more colors per row, creating floats on the wrong side of the fabric. This technique is sometimes called Fair Isle knitting after the traditional Fair Isle patterns that are composed of small motifs with frequent color changes.

To keep an even tension and prevent holes while knitting, pick up yarns alternately over and under one another across or around. While knitting, stretch the stitches on the needle slightly wider than the length of the float at the back to keep work from puckering.

When changing colors at the beginning of rows or rounds, carry yarn along for a few rows only, or cut yarn and rejoin when needed. It is important to keep the floats small and neat so they don't catch on small fingers when the garment is pulled on.

BLOCKING

Blocking is a crucial finishing step in the knitting process. It is the best way to shape pattern pieces and smooth knitted edges in preparation for sewing together. Most garments retain their shape if the blocking stages in the instructions are followed carefully. Choose a blocking method according to the instructions on the yarn care label, and when in doubt, test-block your gauge swatch.

Wet Block Method

Using rust-proof pins, pin pieces to measurements on a flat surface and lightly dampen using a spray bottle. Allow to dry before removing pins.

Steam Block Method

With wrong sides facing, pin pieces. Steam lightly, holding the iron 2"/5cm above the knitting. Do not press or it will flatten stitches.

THREE NEEDLE BIND-OFF

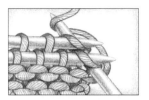

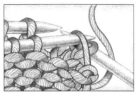

1 With RS placed together, hold pieces on two parallel needles. Insert a third needle knitwise into the first stitch of each needle, and wrap the yarn around the needle as if to knit.

2 Knit these two stitches together, and slip them off the needles. *Knit the next two stitches together in the same manner.

3 Slip the first stitch on the third needle over the second stitch and off the needle. Repeat from the * in Step 2 across the row until all stitches have been bound off.

THE KITCHENER STITCH

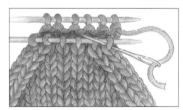

1 Insert tapestry needle purlwise (as shown) through first stitch on front needle. Pull yarn through, leaving that stitch on knitting needle.

2 Insert tapestry needle knitwise (as shown) through first stitch on back needle. Pull yarn through, leaving stitch on knitting needle.

3 Insert tapestry needle knitwise through first stitch on front needle, slip stitch off needle and insert tapestry needle purlwise (as shown) through next stitch on front needle. Pull yarn through, leaving this stitch on needle.

4 Insert tapestry needle purlwise through first stitch on back needle. Slip stitch off needle and insert tapestry needle knitwise (as shown) through next stitch on back needle. Pull yarn through, leaving this stitch on needle.
Repeat steps 3 and 4 until all stitches on both front and back needles have been grafted. Fasten off and weave in end.

Refer to the yarn label for the recommended cleaning method. Many of the projects in the book can be either washed by hand, or in the machine on a gentle or wool cycle, using lukewarm water with a mild detergent. Do not agitate or soak for more than 10 minutes. Rinse gently with tepid water, then fold in a towel and gently press the water out. Lay flat to dry, away from excess heat and light. Check the yarn label for any specific care instructions such as dry cleaning or tumble drying.

KNITTING TERMS AND ABBREVIATIONS

approx approximately

beg begin(ning)

bind off Used to finish an edge and keep stitches from unraveling. Lift the first stitch over the second, the second over the third, etc. (UK: cast off)

cast on A foundation row of stitches placed on the needle in order to begin knitting.

CC contrast color

ch chain(s)

cm centimeter(s)

cont continu(e)(ing)

dc double crochet (UK: tr–treble)

dec decrease(ing)–Reduce the stitches in a row (knit 2 together).

dpn double-pointed needle(s)

foll follow(s)(ing)

g gram(s)

garter stitch Knit every row. Circular knitting: knit one round, then purl one round.

hdc half double crochet (UK: htr–half treble)

YARN SYMBOLS

① **Fine Weight**

(29-32 stitches per 4"/10cm) *Includes baby and fingering yarns, and some of the heavier crochet cottons. The range of needle sizes is 0-4 (2-3.5mm).*

② **Lightweight**

(25-28 stitches per 4"/10cm) *Includes sport yarn, sock yarn, UK 4-ply, and lightweight DK yarns. The range of needle sizes is 3-6 (3.25-4mm).*

③ **Medium Weight**

(21-24 stitches per 4"/10cm) *Includes DK and worsted, the most commonly used knitting yarns. The range of needle sizes is 6-9 (4-5.5mm).*

④ **Medium-heavy Weight**

(17-20 stitches per 4"/10cm) *Also called heavy worsted or Aran. The range of needle sizes is 8-10 (5-6mm).*

⑤ **Bulky Weight**

(13-16 stitches per 4"/10cm) *Also called chunky. Includes heavier Icelandic yarns. The range of needle sizes is 10-11 (6-8mm).*

⑥ **Extra-bulky Weight**

(9-12 stitches per 4"/10cm) *The heaviest yarns available. The range of needle sizes is 11 and up (8mm and up).*

inc increase(ing)–Add stitches in a row (knit into the front and back of a stitch).

k knit

k2tog knit 2 stitches together

LH left-hand

lp(s) loop(s)

m meter(s)

M1 make one stitch–With the needle tip, lift the strand between last stitch worked and next stitch on the left-hand needle and knit into the back of it. One stitch has been added.

MC main color

mm millimeter(s)

no stitch On some charts, "no stitch" is indicated with shaded spaces where stitches have been decreased or not yet made. In such cases, work the stitches of the chart, skipping over the "no stitch" spaces.

oz ounce(s)

p purl

p2tog purl 2 stitches together

pat(s) pattern

pick up and knit (purl) Knit (or purl) into the loops along an edge.

pm place markers–Place or attach a loop of contrast yarn or purchased stitch marker as indicated.

psso pass slip stitch(es) over

rem remain(s)(ing)

rep repeat

rev St st reverse stockinette stitch–Purl right-side rows, knit wrong-side rows. Circular knitting: purl all rounds. (UK: reverse stocking stitch)

rnd(s) round(s)

RH right-hand

RS right side(s)

sc single crochet (UK: dc–double crochet)

sk skip

SKP Slip 1, knit 1, pass slip stitch over knit 1.

SK2P Slip 1, knit 2 together, pass slip stitch over the knit 2 together.

sl slip–An unworked stitch made by passing a stitch from the left-hand to the right-hand needle as if to purl.

sl st slip stitch (UK: sc–single crochet)

ssk slip, slip, knit–Slip next 2 stitches knitwise, one at a time, to right-hand needle. Insert tip of left-hand needle into fronts of these stitches from left to right. Knit them together. One stitch has been decreased.

sssk Slip next 3 sts knitwise, one at a time, to right-hand needle. Insert tip of left-hand needle into fronts of these stitches from left to right. Knit them together. Two stitches have been decreased.

st(s) stitch(es)

St st Stockinette stitch–Knit right-side rows, purl wrong-side rows. Circular knitting: knit all rounds. (UK: stocking stitch)

tbl through back of loop

tog together

WS wrong side(s)

wyib with yarn in back

wyif with yarn in front

work even Continue in pattern without increasing or decreasing. (UK: work straight)

yd yard(s)

yo yarn over–Make a new stitch by wrapping the yarn over the right-hand needle. (UK: yfwd, yon, yrn)

* = Repeat directions following * as many times as indicated.

[ ] = Repeat directions inside brackets as many times as indicated.

For Experienced Knitters

Twisted rib diamonds and bobbles are knit in the Guernsey tradition, then framed by marching rows of numbers and pastel rib-point trimming on the neck and lower edges. Designed by Maggie Branch.

SIZE

Instructions are written for size 2. Changes for sizes 3 and 4 are in parentheses.

KNITTED MEASUREMENTS

- Chest 26 (28, 30)"/66 (71, 76)cm
- Length 12 (13, 14)"/30.5 (33, 35.5)cm
- Upper arm 9 (10, 11)"/23 (25.5, 28)cm

MATERIALS

- 4 (5, 5) 1¾oz/50g balls (each approx 123yd/ 113m) of Rowan/Westminster Fibers *Wool Cotton* (wool/cotton ③) in #900 ecru (MC)
- 1 ball each in #934 lt blue (A), #929 beige (B), #902 rose (C), #932 yellow (D), #901 lt green (E), #904 blue (F), #934 grey blue (G) and #930 sage (H)
- One pair each sizes 3 and 5 (3 and 3.75mm) needles *or size to obtain gauge*
- Bobbins
- Cable needle
- Stitch holder

GAUGES

- 22 sts and 32 rows to 4"/10cm over St st using larger needles.
- 25 sts and 32 rows to 4"/10cm across all sts using larger needles.

Take time to check gauge.

TWO-STITCH CABLE

Row 1 (RS) K2.

Rows 2 and 4 P2.

Row 3 Pass RH needle in *front* of first st, k 2nd st, then k first st and sl both sts from needle tog.

Rep rows 1-4 for two-stitch cable.

DIAMOND BOBBLE PATTERN

over 23 sts

Bobble (MB) K1, p1, k1, p1, k1 into 1 st (for 5 sts). Turn, p5. Pass 2nd, 3rd, 4th and 5th st over first st. K1 tbl in rem st.

2-st RT Sl 1 st to cn and hold to *back*, k1 tbl, then k1 tbl from cn.

2-st RPT Sl 1 st to cn and hold to *back*, k1 tbl, then p1 from cn.

2-st LT Sl 1 st to cn and hold to *front*, k1 tbl, then k1 tbl from cn.

2-st LPT Sl 1 st to cn and hold to *front*, p1, then k1 tbl from cn.

Row 1 (RS) P8, [k1 tbl, p1] 3 times, k1 tbl, p8.

Row 2 K8, [p1, k1] 3 times, p1, k8.

Row 3 P7, [2-st RPT] twice, k1 tbl, [2-st LPT] twice, p7.

Row 4 K7, [p1, k1] 4 times, p1, k7.

Row 5 P6, 2-st RPT, 2-st RT, p1, k1 tbl, p1, 2-st LT, 2-st LPT, p6.

Row 6 K6, p1, k1, p2, k1, p1, k1, p2, k1, p1, k6.

Row 7 P5, [2-st RPT] twice, [k1 tbl, p1] twice, k1 tbl, [2-st LPT] twice, p5.

Row 8 K5, [p1, k1] 6 times, p1, k5.

Row 9 P4, 2-st RPT, 2-st RT, [p1, k1 tbl] 3 times, p1, 2-st LT, 2-st LPT, p4.

Row 10 K4, p1, k1, p2, [k1, p1] 3 times, k1, p2, k1, p1, k4.

Row 11 P3, [2-st RPT] twice, [k1 tbl, p1] 4 times, k1 tbl, [2-st LPT] twice, p3.
Row 12 K3, [p1, k1] 8 times, p1, k3.
Row 13 P2, [2-st RPT] twice, [p1, k1 tbl] 5 times, p1, [2-st LPT] twice, p2.
Row 14 K2, [p1, k1] twice, k1, [p1, k1] 5 times, [k1, p1] twice, k2.
Row 15 P2, [k1 tbl, p1] twice, p1, MB in next st, [p1, k1 tbl] 3 times, p1, MB in next st, p2, k1 tbl, p1, k1 tbl, p2.
Row 16 K2, p1, k1, p1, k4, [p1, k1] twice, p1, k4, p1, k1, p1, k2.
Row 17 P2, [2-st LPT] twice, p3, MB in next st, p1, k1 tbl, p1, MB in next st, p3, [2-st RPT] twice, p2.
Row 18 K3, p1, k1, p1, k5, p1, k5, p1, k1, p1, k3.
Row 19 P3, [2-st LPT] twice, p4, MB in next st, p4, [2-st RPT] twice, p3.
Row 20 K4, p1, k1, p1, k9, p1, k1, p1, k4.
Row 21 P4, [2-st LPT] twice, p7, [2-st RPT] twice, p4.
Row 22 K5, p1, k1, p1, k7, p1, k1, p1, k5.
Row 23 P5, [2-st LPT] twice, p5, [2-st RPT] twice, p5.
Row 24 K6, p1, k1, p1, k5, p1, k1, p1, k6.
Row 25 P6, [2-st LPT] twice, p3, [2-st RPT] twice, p6.
Row 26 K7, p1, k1, p1, k3, p1, k1, p1, k7.
Row 27 P7, [2-st LPT] twice, p1, [2-st RPT] twice, p7.
Row 28 K8, [p1, k1] 3 times, p1, k8.
Rep rows 3-28 for diamond bobble pat.

GARTER STITCH TRIANGLE
With smaller needles, cast on 2 sts.
Row 1 K2.
Row 2 Yo (bring yarn over top and then under to back of needle), k to end. Rep row 2 until there are 10 or 12 sts as indicated for size.

BACK
Note Each triangle is worked in a separate color and then all are joined tog to form edge. Using a different color for each triangle, work as foll: for size 2, make seven 12-st triangles; for size 3, make nine 10-st triangles; for size 4, make eight 12-st triangles. There are a total of 84 (90, 96) sts when all triangles are completed.
Join triangles
Next row (RS) With MC, k across all triangles, dec 1 st—83 (89, 95) sts. Change to larger needles. Work 6 rows in garter st with MC.
Set up pats
Row 1 (RS) P2 (5, 5), 2-st cable, p2, 2-st cable, p2, k12, [p2, 2-st cable] twice, p0 (0, 3), 23-st diamond bobble pat, p0 (0, 3), [2-st cable, p2] twice, k12, [p2, 2-st cable] twice, p2, (5, 5). Cont to foll chart and pats in this way ONLY, working 6 (7, 8) more rows with MC before beg number panels and working 0 (2, 4) more rows with MC in between each number panel (to add length for other sizes) and cont with MC for 7 (8, 9) rows after panels are completed to end of

piece. Cont in this way until piece measures 12 (13, 14)"/30.5 (33, 35.5)cm from beg of points. Bind off.

FRONT

Work as for back until piece measures 9¾ (10¾, 11¾)"/25 (27, 30)cm from beg.

Neck shaping

Next row (RS) Work 30 (33, 34) sts, with separate ball of yarn, bind off 23 (23, 27) sts, work to end. Working both sides at once, dec 1 st from each neck edge every other row 6 times—24 (27, 28) sts rem each side. When same length as back, bind off rem sts each side.

SLEEVES

With smaller needles and MC, cast on 35 (39, 41) sts. Work in garter st for 8 (8, 10) rows. Change to larger needles.

Beg pat st

Row 1 (RS) P6 (8, 9), work 23-st diamond bobble pat, p6 (8, 9). Cont in this way,

inc 1 st each side every 4th row 6 times, every 8th row 3 (4, 6) times—53 (59, 65) sts. Work even until piece measures 7 (7¾, 8½)"/18 (19.5, 21.5)cm from beg. Bind off.

FINISHING

Block pieces to measurements. Sew one shoulder seam.

Neckband

Working different colored triangles as on lower edge, work 7 (7, 9) 12-st (12-st, 10 st) triangles and set aside. With smaller needles and MC, pick up and k 84 (84, 90) sts evenly around neck edge. K 1 row. **Next row (RS)** K tog 1 st of triangle with 1 st of neckband until all triangles are joined. K 2 more rows with MC. Bind off. Sew other shoulder and neckband seam. Place markers at 4½ (5, 5½)"/11.5 (12.5, 14)cm down from shoulders. Sew sleeves to armholes between markers. Sew side and sleeve seams.

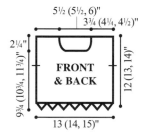

5½ (5½, 6)"
3¾ (4¼, 4½)"
2¼"
9¾ (10¾, 11¾)"
FRONT & BACK
12 (13, 14)"
13 (14, 15)"

9 (10, 11)"
SLEEVE
7 (7¾, 8½)"
5½ (6¼, 6½)"

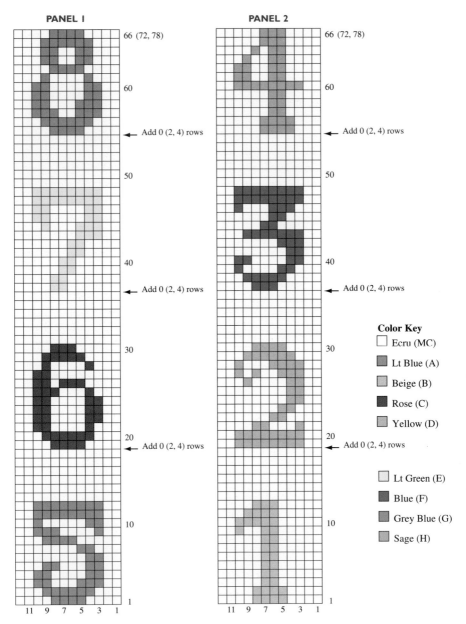

PANEL I

66 (72, 78)

60

← Add 0 (2, 4) rows

50

40

← Add 0 (2, 4) rows

30

20
← Add 0 (2, 4) rows

10

1

11   9   7   5   3   1

PANEL 2

66 (72, 78)

60

← Add 0 (2, 4) rows

50

40

← Add 0 (2, 4) rows

30

20
← Add 0 (2, 4) rows

10

1

11   9   7   5   3   1

Color Key

☐ Ecru (MC)

▨ Lt Blue (A)

▨ Beige (B)

■ Rose (C)

▨ Yellow (D)

☐ Lt Green (E)

■ Blue (F)

▨ Grey Blue (G)

▨ Sage (H)

CABLED VEST
Future investment

This smart vest, with a separated double cable that forms the V-neck trim, is knit in a summery cotton yarn with textured elasticity. Designed by Jil Eaton.

SIZES

Instructions are written for size 2. Changes for sizes 3 and 4 are in parentheses.

KNITTED MEASUREMENTS

▪ Chest 23 (25, 27)"/58.5 (63.5, 68.5)cm
▪ Length 13 (14, 15)"/33 (35.5, 38)cm

MATERIALS

▪ 4 (4, 5) 1¾oz/50g balls (each approx 87yd/80m) of Berroco, Inc. *Smart Cotton* (cotton/rayon/nylon ③) in #1321 blue
▪ One pair size 7 (4.5mm) needles *or size to obtain gauge*
▪ One set (4) size 7 (4.5mm) dpn
▪ Size 7 (4.5mm) circular needle, 16"/40cm long
▪ Cable needle
▪ Stitch holders

GAUGE

21 sts and 30 rows to 4"/10cm over St st using size 7 (4.5mm) needles.
Take time to check gauge.

CABLE PANEL

Over 18 sts.
Rows 1 and 3 (RS) P2, k6, p2, k6, p2.

Row 2 and all even rows K the knit and p the purl sts.
Row 5 P2, sl 3 sts to cn and hold to *back*, k3, k3 from cn, p2, sl 3 sts to cn and hold to *front*, k3, k3 from cn, p2.
Row 7 Rep row 1.
Row 8 Rep row 2.
Rep rows 1-8 for cable panel.

BACK

With straight needles, cast on 61 (65, 71) sts. Work in k1, p1 rib for 3 rows. Cont in St st until piece measures 8 (8½, 9)"/20.5 (21.5, 23)cm from beg.
Armhole shaping
Bind off 3 (3, 4) sts at beg of next 2 rows. Dec 1 st each side every other row 2 (3, 4) times—51 (53, 55) sts. Work even until armhole measures 5 (5½, 6)"/12.5 (14, 15)cm.
Neck and shoulder shaping
Work 12 (13, 13) sts and place on a holder, work 27 (27, 29) sts for back neck and place on a holder, work rem 12 (13, 13) sts and place on a holder.

FRONT

Work rib as for back, inc 5 sts evenly across last WS row—66 (70, 76) sts.
Beg cable panel
Next row (RS) K 24 (26, 29) sts, work 18 sts in cable panel, k 24 (26, 29). Cont in pats as established, working sts each side of cable panel in St st, until same length as back to armhole.

Armhole and neck shaping

Next row (RS) Bind off 3 (3, 4) sts, work to 2 sts before cable panel, k2tog, work 18-st cable panel, SKP, work to end. Cont to shape armhole binding off 3 (3, 4) sts at beg of next row, then dec 1 st every other row 2 (3, 4) times AT SAME TIME, dec 1 st at each neck edge every other row 3 times more.

Separate for V-neck

Next row (RS) Cont armhole decs, work to 2 sts before cable panel, k2tog, p2, k6, p1, join another ball of yarn and p2, k6, p2, SKP, work to end. Cont in this way to dec 1 st at each neck edge every other row 12 (9,10) times more, every 4th row 0 (2, 3) times. Work even until same length as back. Place 12 (13, 13) sts each side on holders for shoulders.

FINISHING

Block pieces to measurements. With WS of pieces tog, sl shoulder sts to 2 dpn. With 3rd dpn, and shoulder sts parallel, k 1 st from back dpn with 1 st from front dpn and bind off while working tog for three-needle bind-off.

Armhole bands

Pick up and k 71 (77, 83) st evenly around each armhole edge. Work in k1, p1 rib for 3 rows. Bind off knitwise.

Neckband

With circular needle, pick up and k 96 (100, 106) sts evenly around neck edge, pm at center V-neck. Work in k1, p1 rib for 3 rows, dec 1 st each side of center V-neck every row. Bind off knitwise. Sew side seams.

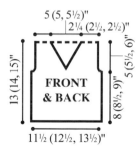

5 (5, 5½)"
2¼ (2½, 2½)"
13 (14, 15)"
8 (8½, 9)"
5 (5½, 6)"

FRONT & BACK

11½ (12½, 13½)"

Raised flower add a colorful trim to this jacket and hat, perfect for a little girl's springtime wardrobe. Rolled edges all around lend a dainty finishing touch. Designed by Irina Poludnenko.

SIZES

Instructions are written for size 4.

KNITTED MEASUREMENTS

- Chest 29"/73.5cm
- Length 13½"/34cm
- Upper arm 11¾"/30cm
- Hat Circumference 17½"/44.5cm

MATERIALS

- 7 1¾oz/50g balls (each approx 108yd/97m) of Tahki•Stacy Charles, Inc. *Cotton Classic* (cotton ④) in #3454 pink (MC)
- 1 ball each in #3001 white (A), #3726 green (B) and #3534 yellow (C)
- One pair size 5 (3.75mm) needles *or size to obtain gauge*
- One set (5) size 5 (3.75mm) dpn
- Size 5 (3.75mm) circular needle, 24"/60cm long
- Stitch holders

GAUGE

19 sts and 26 rows to 4"/10cm over St st using size 5 (3.75mm) needles.
Take time to check gauge.

BACK

With A, cast on 68 sts. Beg with a p row, work in St st for 6½"/16.5cm.

Armhole shaping

Bind off 4 sts at beg of next 2 rows, 3 sts at beg of next 2 rows, 2 sts at beg of next 2 rows, dec 1 st each side on next row— 48 sts. Work even until armhole measures 6½"/16.5cm).

Neck and shoulder shaping

Bind off 5 sts at beg of next 4 rows. Sl rem 28 sts to a holder for back neck.

RIGHT FRONT

With A, cast on 13 sts. P 1 row. Cast on 6 sts at beg of next row and k across. P 1 row. Cont to cast on at beg of each k row 5 sts once, 4 sts once, 3 sts once, 2 sts once and 1 st once—34 sts. Work even until piece measures 6½"/16.5cm from beg.

Armhole shaping

Next row (WS) Bind off 4 sts, purl to end. Cont to bind off from armhole edge 3 sts once, 2 sts once and 1 st once—24 sts. Work even until armhole measures 3½"/9cm.

Neck shaping

Next row (RS) Bind off 3 sts, k to end. Cont to bind off from neck edge 3 sts twice, 2 sts once and 1 st 3 times—10 sts. Work even until same length as back. Shape shoulder at side edge as for back.

LEFT FRONT

Work to correspond to right front, reversing all shaping.

SLEEVES

Note Cuff is made in 2 pieces.
Left side
With A, cast on 10 sts. P 1 row. Cast on 3

sts at beg of next row and k across. P 1 row. Cont to cast on at beg of each k row 2 sts once, 1 st once—16 sts. Lay work aside.

Right side

Work as for left side, only cast on at beg of p rows.

Join pieces

Next row (RS) Beg at straight (unshaped) edge of right side, k16, then k16 sts of left side—32 sts. Inc 1 st each side on next row then every 6th row 11 times more—56 sts. Work even until piece measures 11½"/29cm from beg at inside seam.

Cap shaping

Bind off 4 sts at beg of next 2 rows, 3 sts at beg of next 2 rows, 2 sts at beg of next 2 rows, 1 st at beg of next 2 rows. Bind off 36 sts.

Flower appliqué

(make 3)

Large petal

(make 18 or 6 for each flower)

With A, cast on 5 sts.

 Row 1 (RS) K2, yo, k1, yo, k2—7 sts. **Row 2 and all even rows** Purl. **Row 3** K3, yo, k1, yo, k3—9 sts. **Row 5** K4, yo, k1, yo, k4—11 sts. **Row 7** Ssk, k7, k2tog. **Row 9** Ssk, k5, k2tog. **Row 11** Ssk, k3, k2tog. **Row 13** Ssk, k1, k2tog—3 sts. **Row 15** SK2P. Fasten off last st.

Medium petal

(make 6 for hat)

With A, cast on 5 sts. Work rows 1-4 as for large petal.

Row 5 Rep row 9 of large petal. **Row 7** Rep row 11. **Row 9** Rep row 13. **Row 11** Rep row 15. Fasten off.

Small petal

(make 12 for cardigan or 6 for each flower)

With A, cast on 5 sts.

Work rows 1-4 of large petal.

Row 5 Rep row 13 of large petal.

Row 7 Rep row 15. Fasten off.

Long bobble rope

(make 1 for hat)

With C, cast on 47 sts.

Row 1 *P3, [k1 in front and back of next st] twice for 4 sts, turn. K4, turn. P4, turn. Pass 2nd, 3rd and 4th st over first st (bobble made); rep from *, end p3. There are 11 bobbles. Bind off all sts purlwise.

Short bobble rope

(make 2 for cardigan)

With C, cast on 23 sts. Work as for short bobble rope with 5 bobbles.

Circle cords

Make one 6"/15cm long (for hat) and two 4"/10cm long (for cardigan) With dpn and B, cast on 3 sts, **Next row (RS)** K3. Do not turn. Slide sts to beg of needle to work next row from RS. Bring yarn around to front; rep from * for I-cord. Bind off at desired length.

Block pieces to measurements. Sew shoulder seams. Set in sleeves. Sew side and sleeve seams.

Neckband

With MC, pick up and k 66 sts evenly around neck. Beg with a k row, work in reverse St st for 9 rows. Bind off.

Front and lower band

With circular needle and MC, pick up and k 88 from front center and lower edge, 68 sts from back, 88 sts from other front edge—244 sts. Work as for neckband.

Sleeve bands

With dpn and MC, beg and end at shaped center edge, pick up and k 46 sts along sleeve cuff. Do *not* join, work back and forth in rows, for 9 rows. Bind off. With C, cast on 1 st. **Row 1** [K1 into front and back of st] 3 times—6 sts. **Rows 2 and 4** Purl. **Rows 3 and 5** Knit. **Row 6** [P2tog] 3 times—3 sts. SK2P. Fasten off. **Buttonloop** With dpn and B, cast on 2 sts. Make a 2"/5cm I-cord. Bind off. Sew on button and loop to top of cardigan. Place large petals in a circle at lower edge of cardigan. Sew small petals in between each large petal. Shape short bobble rope in a circle at flower center. Sew circle cord around bobble rope.

HAT

With MC and dpn, cast on 84 sts. Work in St st for 7"/18cm. **Next rnd** [K12, k2tog, pm] 6 times. K 1 rnd. **Next rnd** [K11, k2tog] 6 times—72 sts. K 1 rnd. Cont in this way to dec 6 sts every other rnd, always k2tog before marker, 11 times more—6 sts. Cut yarn and pull through sts and draw up lightly. Sew flowers to center of hat as on cardigan.

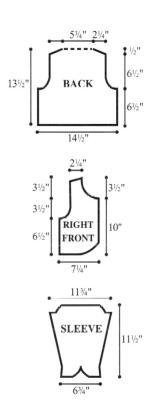

She loves me, she loves me not

An ingenious approach to circular knitting makes this girl's dress fun to knit and construct. It is knit all in one piece with a crossover back and is finished with bias rib edging and an applied flower. Designed by Diane Weitzel.

Instructions are written for size 2.

KNITTED MEASUREMENTS
▪ Chest 22"/56cm
▪ Length 14½"/37cm

MATERIALS
▪ 4 1¾oz/50g balls (each approx 142yd/130m) of Schoeller Esslinger/Skacel Collection *Merino Soft* (wool ③) in #21 lavender (MC)
▪ Small amount of tapestry yarn in dk pink (A), pink (B), gold (C) and green (D)
▪ Size 5 (3.75mm) circular needle, 32"/81cm long *or size to obtain gauge*
▪ One pair size 5 (3.75mm) needles
▪ Stitch markers
▪ Stitch holders

GAUGE
24 sts and 32 rows to 4"/10cm over knot pat st using size 5 (3.75mm) needles. *Take time to check gauge.*

KNOT PATTERN STITCH
(multiple of 4 sts)
Row 1 and all WS rows Purl.
Row 2 (RS) *K2, p2tog leaving st on needle, insert RH needle from back between the 2 sts just purled tog and p the first st again, then sl both sts from needle tog; rep from * to end.

Row 4 *P2tog and p the first st again (as in row 2), k2; rep from * to end. Rep rows 1-4 for knot pat st.

BIAS BAND PATTERN
(over an even number of sts)
Rows 1 and 3 (WS) Purl.
Row 2 (RS) *K2tog but do not sl from LH needle, then insert RH needle between the sts just knitted tog and k the first st again, then sl both sts from needle tog; rep from * to end.
Row 4 K1; rep from * of row 2 to last st, k1. Rep rows 1-4 for bias band pat.

DECREASE SEQUENCE
Decreases are worked each side of markers working over 5 sts before marker and 5 sts after marker (or over 10 sts) as foll:
Dec row (RS) Work to 5 sts before marker, *k1, wyif sl 1 purlwise, p2tog, psso, wyib, k1*; sl marker, rep between *'s once, cont in pat to end. Rep dec row every 6th row as described in instructions.
Notes 1 When beg a RS row after sts are just cast on, first k the cast on sts then beg knot pat st on the foll RS row, ensuring the continuity of pat. **2** Read through instructions carefully before beginning to knit.

BODY
With MC, cast on 10 sts. **Row 1 (WS)** Purl. Turn and cast on 8 sts—18 sts. **Row 2** K8 cast-on sts, beg row 2 of knot pat st over rem sts. Turn and cast on 8 sts—26 sts. **Row 3** Purl. Turn and cast on 8 sts—34 sts. **Row 4** K8 cast-on sts, cont with row 4 of knot pat st over rem sts. Turn and cast on 8 sts—42 sts. Cont to work in this way, working rows 1-4 of knot pat st and

casting on 8 sts at beg of next 4 rows, 42 sts at beg of next 2 rows, 20 sts at beg of next 2 rows, 10 sts at beg of next 2 rows, 4 sts at beg of next 8 rows—250 sts. **Next row (WS)** P67, pm, p116, pm, p67. Turn and cast on 4 sts—254 sts. **Next (dec) row (RS)** Work dec row as described under decrease sequence at each marker (therefore, 8 sts are dec'd in one row). Turn and cast on 4 sts—250 sts. Cont to cast on 2 sts at beg of next 8 rows, then [work straight without casting on for 8 rows, cast on 2 sts at beg of next 2 rows] 4 times, work straight without casting on for 8 rows, AT SAME TIME, work dec row every 6th row a total of 9 times more—210 sts.

Divide for back straps and bodice
Next row (WS) P43, bind off 36 sts, p until there are 52 sts from bind-off, bind off 36, p to end. Turn.

Back strap #1
Next row (RS) Work 43 sts, turn. **Next row** Bind off 7 sts, purl to end. **Next row** Work even. **Next row** Bind off 2 sts, purl to end—34 sts. Rep last 2 rows 7 times more—20 sts. **Next row** Work even. **Next row** Purl, turn. Cast on 2 sts—22 sts. Work 1 row even. **Next row** Bind off 2 sts, purl to end—20 sts. [Work 3 rows even. Bind off 2 sts at beg of next row, p to end] 3 times—14 sts. Work 9 rows even. Cut yarn and place sts on a holder.

BODICE
(over 52 sts)
Next row (RS) Dec 1 st each side of row—50 sts. Work 14 rows even.

Neck shaping
Next row (WS) P20, join a 2nd ball of yarn and bind off 10 sts, p to end. Working both sides at once, bind off 2 sts from each neck edge twice. Work even for 12 rows. Bind off 2 sts from each neck edge once—14 sts each side. Work even for 9 rows or until same length as back. Sl rem sts each side to holders.

Back strap #2
Work as for back strap #1, reversing shaping by binding off on opposite edge.

FINISHING
Crossing over shoulders at back, block piece to measurements. Graft tog shoulders using Kitchener st.

Bias band
With MC, cast on 10 sts. Work bias band pat until piece measures 129"/327cm slightly stretched. With WS of band to RS of dress, pin band around entire outer neck and armhole edges of dress. Sew in place, adjusting band length if necessary and then binding off. Fold band up to RS and sew to dress encasing all edges (see photo).

FLOWER APPLIQUÉ
Petal
With B cast on 5 sts. **Row 1 (RS)** Knit. **Rows 2, 4, 6, 8 and 10** Purl. **Rows 3, 5 and 7** K in front and back of first st, k to last st, k in front and back of last st—11 sts after row 7. **Row 9** Dec 1 st each end of row—9 sts. Change to A and rep row 9—7 sts. **Row 11** P2tog, p3, p2tog—5 sts. Leave sts on needle. Work 6 more petals in same way, leaving all sts of petal on needle. Cut yarn leaving a 12"/30cm end.

Draw through all 35 sts on needle and pull tightly to fasten into circle. Block flower and sew to dress front.

Center

With C, cast on 1 st. K into front, back, front, back and front of st, turn. P5, turn. K5, turn. P5, pass the 2nd, 3rd, 4th and 5th st over first st. Fasten off. Sew to flower center.

Leaves

(make 2)

With D, cast on 5 sts. **Row 1 (RS)** K2, yo, k1, yo, k2—7 sts. **Row 2 and all even rows** Purl. **Row 3** K3, yo, k1, yo, k3—9 sts. **Row 5** K4, yo, k1, yo, k4—11 sts. **Row 7** Ssk, k7, k2tog—9 sts. **Row 9** Ssk, k5, k2tog—7 sts. **Row 11** Ssk, k3, k2tog—5 sts. **Row 13** Ssk, k1, k2tog—3 sts. **Row 15** SK2P. Fasten off last st. Block leaves and sew to each side of flower.

Flower appliqué is from *Knitted Embellishments* by Nicky Epstein.

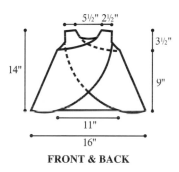

FRONT & BACK

Very Easy Very Vogue

Garter-stitch ridges punctuate stripes in pink or blue hues for your favorite little girl or boy. Simple seed stitch edges finish both styles, designed by Charlotte Parry.

SIZES
Instructions are written for size 2. Changes for sizes 3 and 4 are in parentheses.

KNITTED MEASUREMENTS
- Chest 22½ (24, 26)"/57 (61, 66)cm
- Length 11½ (12½, 13½)"/29 (32, 34)cm
- Upper arm 10 (11, 12)"/25 (28, 30)cm

MATERIALS
Pullover
- 2 (2, 2) 3½oz/100g balls (each approx 215yd/ 197m) of Brown Sheep Co. *Cotton Fleece* (cotton/wool ④) in #CW-585 navy (MC)
- 1 (1, 1) ball each in #CW-360 green (A), #CW-380 lt green (B) and #CW-570 lt blue (C)

Cardigan
- 2 (2, 2) balls in #CW-800 purple (MC)
- 1 (1, 1) ball each in #CW-680 yellow (A), #CW-690 lilac (B) and #CW-230 pink (C)
- One pair each sizes 5 and 6 (3.75 and 4mm) needles *or size to obtain gauge*
- Size 5 (3.75mm) circular needle, 16"/40cm long
- Five ⅝"/15mm buttons

GAUGE
22 sts and 34 rows to 4"/10cm over stripe pat st using larger needles.
Take time to check gauge.

STRIPE PATTERN STITCH
*Work 4 rows in St st with A, k 2 rows MC, 4 rows in St st with B, k 2 rows MC, 4 rows in St st with C, k 2 rows MC; rep from * (18 rows) for stripe pat.

SEED STITCH
(over an even number of sts)
Row 1 *K1, p1; rep from * to end.
Row 2 K the purl and p the knit sts.
Rep row 2 for seed st.

BACK
With smaller needles and MC, cast on 62 (66, 71) sts. Work in seed st for 6 rows. Change to larger needles and cont in stripe pat until piece measures 11½ (12½, 13½)"/29 (32, 34)cm from beg. Bind off.

SLEEVES
With smaller needles and MC, cast on 30 (32, 34) sts. Work in seed st for 6 rows. Change to larger needles and cont in stripe pat, inc 1 st each side every 4th row 5 (6, 8) times, every 6th row 8 times—56 (60, 66) sts. Work even until piece measures 10½ (11, 11½)"/26.5 (28, 29)cm from beg, end with 2 rows in MC. Bind off.

PULLOVER
FRONT
Work as for back until piece measures 9½ (10½, 11½)"/24 (26.5, 29)cm.

Neck shaping
Next row (RS) Work 26 (28, 30) sts, join another ball of yarn and bind off center 10 (10, 11) sts, work to end. Working both

sides at once, bind off 3 sts from each neck edge once, 2 sts once, dec 1 st every other row twice. When same length as back, bind off rem 19 (21, 23) sts each side for shoulders.

CARDIGAN
LEFT FRONT

With smaller needles and MC, cast on 28 (30, 33) sts. Work in seed st for 6 rows. Change to larger needles and cont in stripe pat until piece measures 9½ (10½, 11½)"/24 (26.5, 29)cm from beg.

Neck shaping

Next row (WS) Bind off 3 sts, work to end. Cont to shape neck, binding off 2 sts from neck edge twice, dec 1 st every other row twice. When same length as back, bind off rem 19 (21, 23) sts for shoulder.

RIGHT FRONT

Work to correspond to left front, reversing all shaping.

FINISHING

Block pieces to measurements. Sew shoulder seams.

PULLOVER
Neckband

With RS facing, circular needle and MC, pick up and k 64 (64, 68) sts evenly around neck edge. Join and work in seed st for 1"/2.5cm. Bind off in pat. Place markers at 5 (5½, 6)"/12.5 (14, 15)cm down from shoulders. Sew sleeves to armholes between markers. Sew side and sleeve seams.

CARDIGAN
Neckband

With smaller needles and MC, pick up and k 61 (61, 65) sts evenly around neck edge. Work in seed st for 1"/2.5cm. Bind off in pat. Place markers at 5 (5½, 6)"/12.5 (14, 15)cm down from shoulders. Sew sleeves to armholes between markers. Sew side and sleeve seams.

Buttonband

With smaller needles and MC, pick up and k 57 (63, 69) sts along left front edge. Work in seed st for 1"/2.5cm. Bind off. Place markers for 5 buttons evenly spaced along band. Work buttonhole band along right front to correspond, working buttonholes opposite each marker on the 3rd row by yo and k2tog. Sew on buttons.

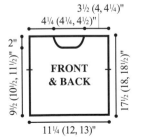

3½ (4, 4¼)"
4¼ (4¼, 4½)"

2"

FRONT & BACK

9½ (10½, 11½)"

17½ (18, 18½)"

11¼ (12, 13)"

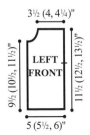

3½ (4, 4¼)"

LEFT FRONT

9½ (10½, 11½)"

11½ (12½, 13½)"

5 (5½, 6)"

10 (11, 12)"

SLEEVE

10½ (11, 11½)"

5½ (5¾, 6)"

These fun-to-knit pillows with heart, hand or foot motifs are sure to be the stars of your favorite toddler's room. Worked in three different colorways, these pillows are knit entirely from a shaped chart. Designed by Mags Kandis.

SIZE

Finished size is approx 19"/48cm tall x 14"/48cm wide.

MATERIALS

- 3 1¾oz/50g balls (each approx 84yd/77m) of Mission Falls *1824 Cotton* (cotton ④) in #201 coral (A) or #406 purple (A) or #204 gold (A)
- 1 ball in #302 olive (B) or #201coral (B) or #406 purple (B)
- One pair size 7 (4.5mm) needles *or size to obtain gauge*
- Size F (4mm) crochet hook
- Stitch holder
- Polyester fiberfill for stuffing

GAUGE

18 sts and 24 rows to 4"/10cm over St st using size 4 (4.5mm) needles. *Take time to check gauge.*

FRONT

Beg at left edge of chart with A, cast on 4 sts. Cont to foll chart with incs, decs, cast-ons and bind-offs as indicated for chosen motif. Bind off last 4 sts at end of star.

BACK

Work as for front, omitting motif.

FINISHING

Block pieces so that edges are flat. Baste front and back tog. With crochet hook and A, join front and back tog by working 1 backwards sc (working from left to right) through both thicknesses, leaving one seam open. Stuff pillow and complete crochet finishing.

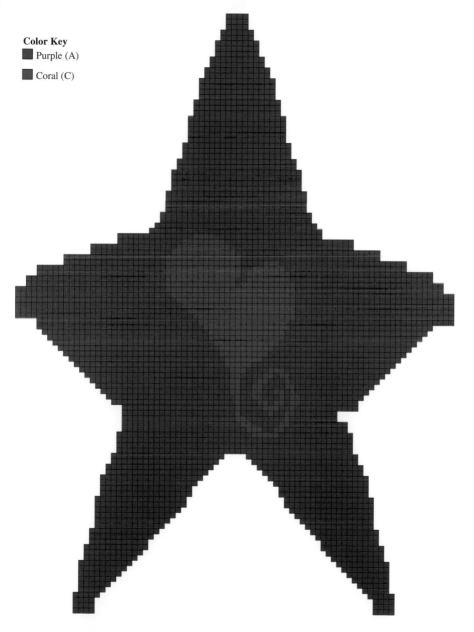

Color Key
- Purple (A)
- Coral (C)

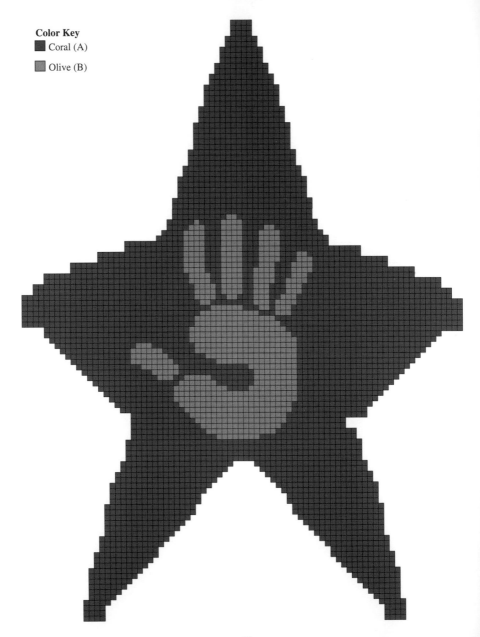

Color Key
- Coral (A)
- Olive (B)

Color Key
- Gold (A)
- Purple (B)

Weekend warrior

Very Easy Very Vogue

Rugged tweed yarn and traditional sweatshirt styling team up for a winning sports combination in this sweatshirt. A patch flap pocket provides a twist on the traditional kangaroo pocket. Designed by Mari Lynn Patrick.

SIZES

Instructions are written for size 2. Changes for sizes 3 and 4 are in parentheses.

KNITTED MEASUREMENTS

 Chest 27 (29, 32)"/68.5 (73.5, 81)cm
 Length 13½ (14½, 15)"/34 (37, 38)cm
 Upper arm 11½ (12½, 13½)"/29 (32, 34)cm

MATERIALS

 2 (2, 2) 8½oz/250g hanks (each approx 525yd/ 484m) of Wool Pak Yarns NZ/Baabajoes Wool Co. *Yarn 8-Ply* (wool ④) in #21 heather
 One pair each sizes 5 and 6 (3.75 and 4mm) needles *or size to obtain gauge*
 Size 6 (4mm) circular needle, 16"/40cm long
 Two size 6 (4mm) dpn
 Size F/5 (4mm) crochet hook
 One ½"/13mm button

GAUGE

21 sts and 28 rows to 4"/10cm over St st using larger needles.
Take time to check gauge.

BACK

With larger needles, cast on 63 (69, 77) sts. Work in St st for 5 rows, inc 8 sts evenly on last RS row—71 (77, 85) sts. K next row on WS for turning ridge. Cont in St st until piece measures 13½ (14½, 15)"/34 (37, 38)cm above turning ridge. Bind off.

FRONT

Work as for back through turning ridge. K 1 row, p 1 row.
Eyelet row (RS) K30 (32, 37), yo, k2tog, k7, k2tog, yo, k30 (33, 37). Cont in St st until piece measures 11 (12, 12½)"/28 (30.5, 32)cm above turning ridge.
Neck shaping
Next row (RS) K28 (31, 34), join another ball of yarn and bind off center 15 (15, 17) sts for neck, work to end. Working both sides at once, bind off 2 sts from each neck edge twice, dec 1 st every other row 3 times—21 (28, 31) sts rem each side. When same length as back, bind off rem sts each side for shoulders.

SLEEVES

With smaller needles, cast on 34 (37, 40) sts.
Row I (RS) P1, *k2, p1; rep from * to end. Cont in k2, p1 rib until piece measures 1"/2.5cm from beg. Change to larger needles and cont in St st, inc 1 st each side every 4th row 13 (14, 15) times—60 (65, 70) sts. Work even until piece measures 10½"/26.5cm from beg. Bind off.

FRONT POCKET

With larger needles, cast on 32 sts. K 1 row. **Next row** Purl, inc 1 st each side of row. K 1 row. Rep last 2 rows 3 times more—40 sts. Work even until pocket measures 5"/12.5cm from cast-on edge. Bind off. With RS facing and crochet hook, work an edge of sc evenly around 3 outer edges of pocket.

POCKET FLAP

With larger needles, cast on 28 sts. K 1 row. **Next row** Purl, inc 1 st each side of row. Rep last 2 rows 5 times more—40 sts. Work even until piece measures 2½"/6.5cm from cast-on edge. Bind off. With crochet hook, work an edge of sc around shaped edge of flap, forming a ch-5 buttonloop at center.

FINISHING

Block pieces to measurements. Sew shoulder seams.

HOOD

With circular needle, beg at center front neck, pick up and k 40 (40, 42) sts to center back neck, pm and pick up center back st, pick up and k 40 (40, 42) sts to end—81 (81, 83) sts. Do *not* join. Working back and forth in rows, k next WS row (for ridge). Cont in St st until hood measures 8 (8½, 9)"/20.5 (21.5, 23)cm.

Top shaping

Next row (RS) K to 2 sts before center marked st, ssk, k1, k2tog, k to end. P 1 row. Rep last 2 rows 6 times more—67 (67, 69) sts. Bind off. Sew top of hood seam.

Hood facing

From RS with circular needle, pick up and k 71 (75, 79) sts evenly around hood opening. K 1 row on WS for turning ridge. Cont in St st for 6 rows more. Bind off . Fold facing to WS at turning ridge and sew in place. Place markers at 5¾ (6¼, 6¾)"/14.5 (16, 17)cm down from shoulders. Sew sleeves to armholes between markers. Center pocket at 4"/10cm above turning ridge. Sew on pocket and sew pocket flap over pocket. Sew on button. Sew side and sleeve seams. Fold hem at lower edge of body to WS at turning ridge and sew in place.

I-CORD

With 2 dpn, cast on 2 sts. ***Row 1** K2. Slide sts to beg of needle and bring yarn around to knit. Rep from * until I-cord measures 36"/92cm. Bind off. Weave cord through eyelets at center front and knot each end.

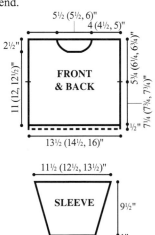

SAILOR PULLOVER
Nautical but nice

Two identical ducks with felt sailor caps decorate a nautical pullover designed by Amy Bahrt. Three buttons run along one shoulder, and the blue stripes are defined in a ridge stitch.

SIZES

Instructions are written for size 2. Changes for sizes 3 and 4 are in parentheses.

KNITTED MEASUREMENTS

- Chest 24 (26, 28)"/61 (66, 71)cm
- Length 13 (14, 15)"/33 (35.5, 38)cm
- Upper arm 10¾ (11½, 12)"/27 (29, 30.5)cm

MATERIALS

- 3 (3, 4) 1¾oz/50g hanks (each approx 108yd/100m) of Tahki•Stacy Charles, Inc. *Cotton Classic* (cotton ④) in #3874 blue (A)
- 4 (4, 5) hanks in #3001 white (B)
- 1 hank each in #3488 red (C) and #3549 yellow (D)
- One pair size 6 (4mm) needles *or size to obtain gauge*
- Three ½"/13mm buttons
- Small amounts of red and white felt
- Bobbins

GAUGES

- 20 sts and 24 rows to 4"/10cm over St st using size 6 (4mm) needles.
- 20 sts and 30 rows to 4"/10cm over stripe pat using size 6 (4mm) needles.
Take time to check gauges.

Note Wind B and C onto bobbins. Work each duck motif with separate bobbins.

BACK

With A, cast on 60 (64, 70) sts. Work in garter st for 1"/2.5cm. Then cont in St st for 32 rows more. *With B, work 4 rows in St st. With A, k 2 rows. Rep from * (6 rows) for stripe pat until piece measures 13 (14, 15)"/33 (35.5, 38)cm from beg, end with 4 rows in B. Bind off 16 (17, 20) sts for shoulder, place center 28 (30, 30) sts on a holder for neck, bind off rem sts for shoulder.

FRONT

Work as for back until 2 rows have been worked above garter band in St st.
Beg chart
Row 1 (RS) Work 9 (11, 13) sts with A, work 16 sts of chart, 10 (10, 12) sts with A, 16 sts of chart, 9 (11, 13) sts with A. Cont as established through row 30 of chart. Then cont in 6-row stripe pat as on back until piece measures 10½ (11½, 12½)"/26.5 (29, 32)cm from beg.
Neck shaping
Next row (RS) Work 25 (27, 29) sts, join another ball of yarn and bind off center 10 (12, 12) sts, work to end. Working both sides at once, bind off 3 sts from each neck edge twice, dec 1 st each side every other row 3 times. When same length as back, bind off rem sts each side for shoulders.

SLEEVES

With B, cast on 34 (36, 36) sts. Work in garter st for 1"/2.5cm. Then cont in 6-row stripe pat, inc 1 st each side every 6th row 10 (11, 12) times—54 (58, 60) sts. Work even until piece measures 10 (10½, 11)"/25.5 (26.5, 28)cm from beg, end with 4 rows in B. Bind off.

FINISHING

Block pieces to measurements. Sew right shoulder seam.

Neckband

With B, pick up and k 72 (76, 76) sts evenly around neck edge. Work in k1, p1 rib for 1¼"/3cm. Bind off in rib. Sew other shoulder

seam. Sew on 3 decorative buttons to front shoulder at ½"/1cm down from seam.

Duck motifs

Cut 2 red felt berets foll template and 2 small streamers in white felt for each hat. Sew with thread to top of ducks' heads on angle as shown. With A, work a French knot for each eye.

Wings (2)

With B, cast on 7 sts. Work in St st for 4 rows. Dec 1 st each side every other row 3 times. Fasten off last st. Sew top of wings to ducks as shown. Place markers at 5¼ (5½, 6)"/13.5 (14, 15)cm down from shoulders. Sew sleeves to armholes between markers. Sew side and sleeve seams.

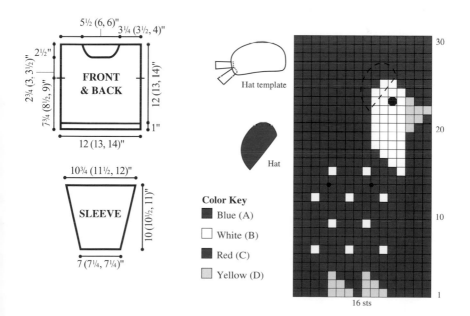

5½ (6, 6)"
3¼ (3½, 4)"

2½"

2¾ (3, 3½)"

7¾ (8½, 9)"

FRONT & BACK

12 (13, 14)"

1"

12 (13, 14)"

10¾ (11½, 12)"

SLEEVE

10 (10½, 11)"

7 (7¼, 7¼)"

Hat template

Hat

Color Key

■ Blue (A)

□ White (B)

■ Red (C)

□ Yellow (D)

30

20

10

1

16 sts

TARTAN COAT

Mad about plaid

This adorable A-line designer plaid coat is edged with corded black trim all around, making it a must for the fashion-conscious little girl. Designed by Mari Lynn Patrick.

SIZES

Instructions are written for size 2. Changes for sizes 3 and 4 are in parentheses.

KNITTED MEASUREMENTS

- Lower edge 37 (39, 41)"/94 (99, 104)cm
- Chest (buttoned) 28 (30, 31½)"/71 (76, 80)cm
- Length 19 (20½, 22)"/48 (52, 56)cm
- Upperarm 11 (11¾, 12¼)"/28 (29, 31)cm

MATERIALS

- 3 (3, 4) 1¾oz/50g balls (each approx 184yd/170m) of GGH/Muench Yarns *Merino Soft* (wool ②) in #15 black (A)
- 3 balls in #3 ecru (B)
- 1 ball in #11 red (C)
- 2 (3, 3) balls in #42 tan (D)
- One pair each sizes 3, 4 and 5 (3, 3.5 and 3.75mm) needles *or size to obtain gauge*
- Size 3 (3mm) circular needle 24"/60cm long
- Four ¾"/20mm buttons
- Bobbins
- Stitch markers

GAUGE

28 sts and 32 rows to 4"/10cm over plaid pat foll chart using size 5 (3.75mm) needles. *Take time to check gauge.*

Note Carry yarn across back of vertical stripes in A and B only. All other blocks or segments of plaid pat should be worked with separate balls or bobbins.

BACK

With size 3 (3mm) needles and A, cast on 132 (138, 144) sts. Work in St st for 5 rows. K next row on WS for turning ridge. Change to size 5 (3.75mm) needles.

Beg plaid chart

Row 1 (RS) K1 (selvage st), work sts 7 (4, 1) through 38 once, then work 28-st rep 3 times, work sts 11 through 24 (27, 30) once, k1 (selvage st). Cont to foll chart in this way (rep rows 1-30), for 18 rows. **Dec row (RS)** K1, SKP, work to last 3 sts, k2tog, k1. Rep dec row every 6th row 4 times, every 4th row 9 (8, 7) times, every 8th row 2 (3, 4) times—100 (106, 112) sts. Work even until piece measures 13 (14, 15)"/33 (35.5, 38)cm from turning ridge.

Armhole shaping

Bind off 6 sts at beg of next 2 rows, 3 sts at beg of next 2 rows, 2 sts at beg of next 4 rows. Dec 1 st each side every other row 2 (2, 3) times—70 (76, 80) sts. Work even until armhole measures 5¼ (5¾, 6¼)"/13.5 (14.5, 16)cm.

Neck and shoulder shaping

Bind off 6 (7, 7) sts at beg of next 6 (6, 2) rows, 8 sts at beg of next 0 (0, 4) rows. Bind off rem 34 sts for back neck.

LEFT FRONT

With size 3 (3mm) needles and A, cast on 75 (78, 81) sts. Work hem as on back. Change to size 5 (3.75mm) needles.

Beg plaid chart

Row 1 (RS) K1 (selvage st), work sts 7 (4, 1) through 38 once, then 28-st rep once, work sts 11-23 once, k1 (selvage st). Cont to foll chart in this way for 18 rows. Dec 1 st at beg of next RS row as on back (side seam), then rep dec every 6th row 4 times, every 4th row 9 (8, 7) times, every 8th row 2 (3, 4) times—59 (62, 65) sts. Work even until same length as back to armhole.

Armhole shaping

From armhole edge, bind off 6 sts once, 3 sts once, 2 sts twice, dec 1 st every other row 2 (2, 3) times—44 (47, 49) sts. Work even until armhole measures $3\frac{1}{4}$ ($3\frac{3}{4}$, $4\frac{1}{4}$)"/8 (9.5, 11)cm, end with a RS row.

Neck shaping

Next row (WS) Bind off 7 sts (neck edge), work to end. Cont to bind off from neck 4 sts once, 3 sts twice, 2 sts 4 times, 1 st once and AT SAME TIME, when same length as back, shape shoulder at side edge as for back.

Work as for left front, reversing shaping and plaid pat and forming 3 buttonholes, the first one at $9\frac{1}{2}$ (11, $12\frac{1}{2}$)"/24 (28, 32)cm from lower edge and the other 3 spaced at 2"/5cm intervals, as foll:

Buttonhole row (RS) Work to last 6 sts, bind off 2 sts, work to end. On next row, cast on 2 sts over bound-off sts.

With size 3 (3mm) needles and A, cast on 48 (50, 52) sts. Work hem as on back. Change to size 5 (3.75mm) needles.

Beg plaid chart

Row 1 (RS) K1 (selvage st), work sts 7 (6, 5) through 38 once, then sts 11-24 (25, 26) once, k1 (selvage st). Cont to foll chart in this way, inc 1 st each side every 8th row once, then every alternate 2nd and 4th row a total of 15 (16, 17) times more—80 (84, 88) sts. Work even until piece measures $8\frac{1}{2}$

($9\frac{1}{2}$, $10\frac{1}{2}$)"/21.5 (24, 26.5)cm from beg.

Cap shaping

Bind off 6 sts at beg of next 2 rows, 3 sts at beg of next 2 rows, 2 sts at beg of next 16 (18, 20) rows, 4 sts at beg of next 4 rows. Bind off rem 14 sts.

Block pieces to measurements. Sew shoulder seams. Turn hems to WS and sew in place.

Left front facing

With size 3 (3mm) needles and A, pick up and k 106 (115, 125) sts evenly along left front edge. K 1 row, p 1 row. Bind off 5 sts (at lower edge), then p to end. [K 1 row, p 1 row] twice. K 1 row. Bind off. Work right front facing in same way, binding off last 5 sts on 3rd row for lower hem.

Neckband

With size 3 (3mm) needles and A, pick up and k 37 sts along right front neck, 34 sts from back neck and 37 sts along left front neck—108 sts. **Row 1 (WS)** K8, work k1, p1 rib to last 8 sts, k8. **Row 2** P8, rib to last 8 sts, p8.

Beg plaid pat

Next row (RS) Bind off 8 sts knitwise, beg with st 12 on row 1, work through st 38, then work 28-st rep twice, work sts 11-19 once, then with separate length of A, bind off last 8 sts. Cont to foll chart rows 1-8. Then change to size 4 (3.5mm) needles and cont to foll chart through row 17. Bind off.

Collar trims

With circular needle and A, pick up and k 12 sts along one side of collar, pm, 92 sts along long edge, pm, 12 sts along other edge. **Next row (WS)** Knit, inc 1 st each side of marker on collar points. Purl 1 row, inc each side of markers as before. Bind off knitwise. Fold facings to WS and sew in place. Sew sleeves into armholes. Sew side and sleeve seams. Sew on buttons.

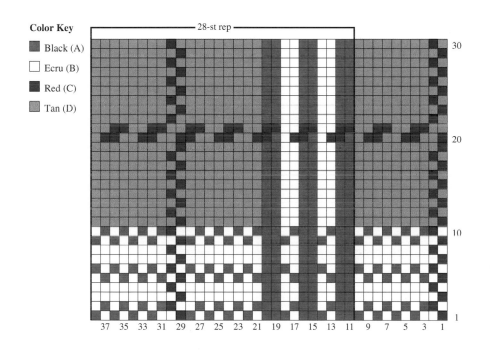

Color Key
- ■ Black (A)
- □ Ecru (B)
- ■ Red (C)
- ▨ Tan (D)

28-st rep

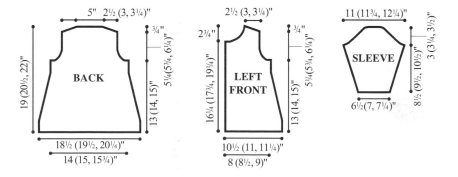

HOODED ONESIE

Romper room

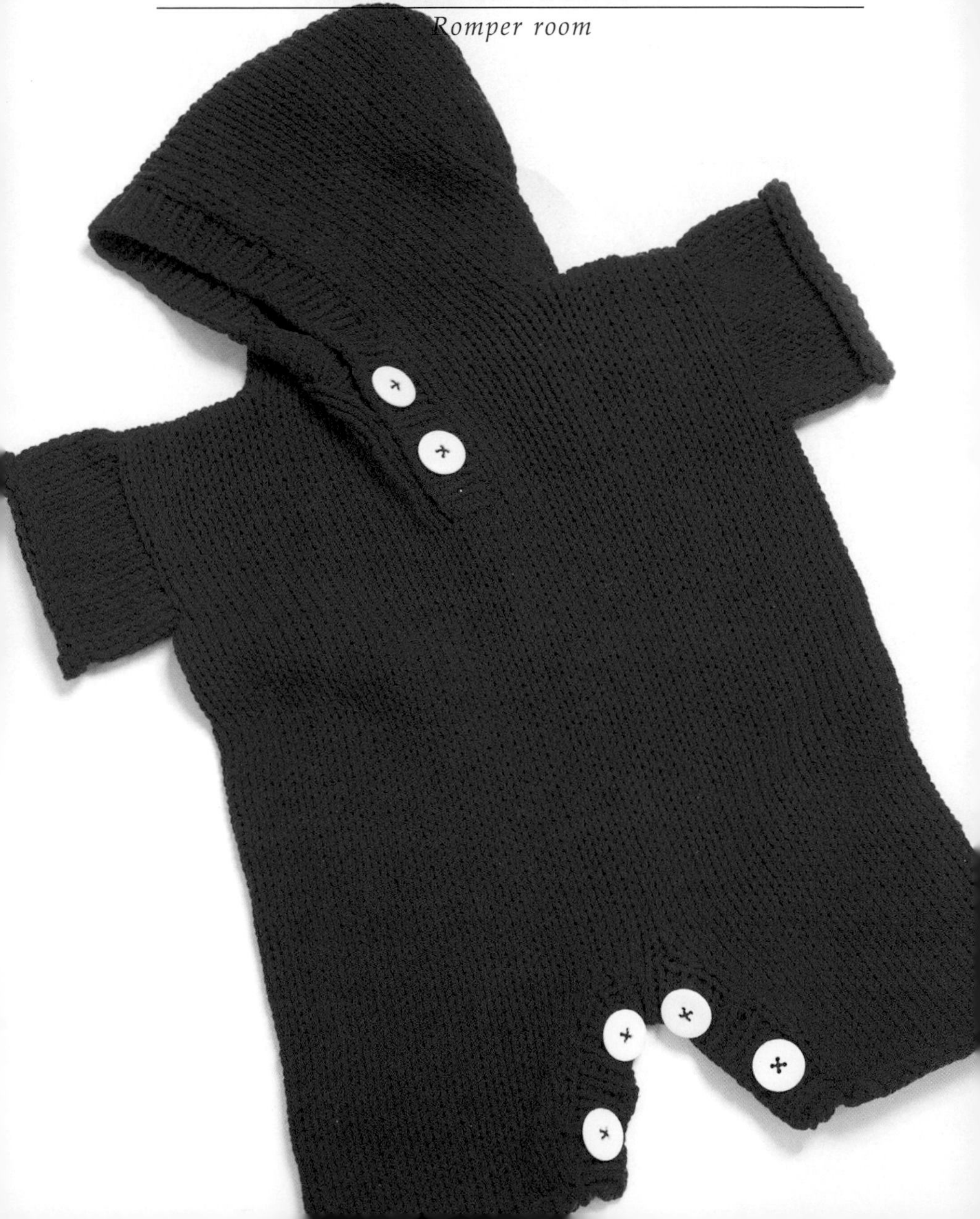

Norah Gaughan's easy-to-knit romper is knit in rounds eliminating all seams except for those at the shoulders. Self-rolling edges and great big buttons finish this simple but playful piece.

SIZES

Instructions are written for size 2. Changes for sizes 3 and 4 are in parentheses.

KNITTED MEASUREMENTS

■ Chest 28 (30, 32)"/71 (76, 81)cm
■ Length 20 (21, 22)"/51 (53, 56)cm
■ Upper arm 10 (11, 12)"/25 (28, 30)cm

MATERIALS

■ 4 (4, 5) 3½/100g balls (each approx 135yd/121m) of Reynolds/JCA *Cabana* (cotton/nylon ⑤) in #913 brick red
■ One each sizes 8 and 10 (5 and 6mm) circular needle, 16"/40cm long *or size to obtain gauge*
■ 1 set (4) size 8 (5mm) dpn
■ Six 1"/25mm buttons

GAUGE

13 sts and 20 rows/rnds to 4"/10cm over St st using larger needles.
Take time to check gauge.

LEGS

(make 2)
With larger circular needle, cast on 36 (40, 42) sts. Working back and forth in rows, work in St st, inc 1 st each side every 6th row 4 times—44 (48, 50) sts. Work even until piece measures 5"/12.5cm from beg. Cast on 3 sts at beg of next RS row and leave sts on needle for crotch.

BODY

After working both legs in the same way, k across sts of first leg then sts of 2nd leg—94 (102, 106) sts. Join all sts to work in rnds. Pm at beg of rnd. Work even until piece measures 10 (10½, 11)"/25.5 (26.5, 28)cm above crotch.

Divide for front and back

Next row (RS) Bind off 3 sts (for center front), work until there are 22 (24, 25) sts for right front, join new yarn and work 47 (51, 53) sts for back, join new yarn and work rem 22 (24, 26) sts for left front. Working back and forth in rows, work even on all pieces at once until armhole measures 5 (5½, 6)"/12.5 (14, 15)cm, end with a WS row.

HOOD

Next row (RS) Work 12 sts of right front, sl 10 (12, 13) sts to dpn for front shoulder, sl first 10 (12, 13) sts on back needle to dpn for back shoulder, bind off these sts tog using 3-needle bind off, then pick up and k 1 st in shoulder, work next 27 sts on back needle for back neck, work next 10 (12, 13) sts on back needle tog with 10 (12, 13) sts on left front needle for shoulders as before, pick up and k 1 st in shoulder, work to end—53 sts. Working back and forth in rows, work in St st until hood measures 8½

(9, 9½)"/21.5 (23, 24)cm. Using Kitchener st, weave sts tog to close hood.

SLEEVES

With dpn, pick up and k 35 (38, 41) sts evenly around armhole opening. Join, dividing sts evenly on 3 dpn. Work in rnds of St st until sleeve measures 3"/7.5cm. Bind off.

FINISHING

Block lightly to measurements.

Back crotch rib

With smaller needles, pick up and k 41 sts along back leg edges, leaving the first and last ½"/1.5cm free for rolled edge. Work in k1, p1 rib for 1"/2.5cm. Bind off. Place markers for 4 buttons evenly spaced. Work front crotch rib in same way forming 4 buttonholes in center by binding off 2 sts for each buttonhole on first row and casting on 2 sts over previous bound-off sts on next row.

Hood rib

With smaller circular needle, pick up and k 93 (97, 103) sts evenly around hood edge. Work in k1, p1 rib, forming 2 buttonholes on left side, the first one at 1½"/4cm from placket opening and the 2nd spaced at a 2"/5cm interval. When band measures 1"/2.5cm, bind off in rib. Sew on buttons.

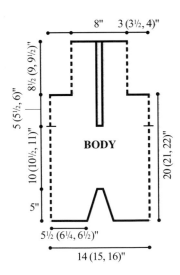

8"   3 (3½, 4)"

8½ (9, 9½)"

5 (5½, 6)"

10 (10½, 11)"

BODY

20 (21, 22)"

5"

5½ (6¼, 6½)"

14 (15, 16)"

For Intermediate Knitters

A simple heart design is repeated in ribbon-like stripes in this bulky knit child's cardigan. Seed-stitch edges, a pointed collar, and novelty square buttons complete the look. Designed by Jean Guirguis.

SIZES
Instructions are written for size 2. Changes for sizes 3 and 4 are in parentheses.

KNITTED MEASUREMENTS
- Chest 22½ (24½, 26)"/57 (62, 66)cm
- Length 10½ (12, 13½)"/26.5 (30.5, 34)cm
- Upper arm 10½ (11½, 12½)"/27 (29, 32)cm

MATERIALS
- 1 3½oz/100g skein (each approx 135yd/124m) of Manos del Uruguay/ Design Source *Manos* (wool ④) each in #R orange (A), #40 gold (B), #10 red (C), #45 blue (D), #46 green (E) and #S purple (F)
- One pair size 9 (5.5mm) needles *or size to obtain gauge*
- Five ½"/13mm square buttons

GAUGE
17 sts and 21 rows to 4"/10cm over St st foll chart using size 9 (5.5mm) needles. *Take time to check gauge.*

BACK
With A, cast on 48 (52, 56) sts. **Row 1 (RS)** *K1, p1; rep from * to end. **Row 2 K** the purl and p the knit sts. Rep row 2 for seed st pat for 1"/2.5cm.

Beg chart pat
Row 1 (RS) Work 3 (2, 1) sts with B, work 6-st rep 7 (8, 9) times, work 3 (2, 1) sts with B. Cont in pat as established, rep rows 1-24, until piece measures 10½ (12, 13½)"/26.5 (30.5, 34)cm from beg. Bind off.

LEFT FRONT
With A, cast on 22 (24, 26) sts. Work in seed st pat for 1"/2.5cm.

Beg chart pat
Row 1 (RS) Work 2 (3, 1) sts with B, work 6-st rep 3 (3, 4) times, work 2 (3, 1) sts with B. Cont in pat as established until piece measures 7½ (9, 10½)"/19 (23, 26.5)cm from beg.

Neck shaping
Next row (WS) Bind off 2 (2, 3) sts, work to end. Cont to shape neck binding off 2 sts from neck edge every other row 3 times. When same length as back, bind off rem 14 (16, 17) sts for shoulder.

RIGHT FRONT
Work to correspond to left front, reversing shaping.

SLEEVES
With A, cast on 28 (30, 32) sts. Work in seed st pat for 1"/2.5cm.

Beg chart pat
Row 1 (RS) Work 2 (3, 1) sts with B, work, 6-st rep 4 (4, 5) times, work 2 (3, 1) sts with B. Cont in pat as established, inc 1 st each

side (working incs into chart pat when there are sufficient sts), every 4th row 8 (9, 11) times—44 (48, 54) sts. Work even until piece measures 8½ (10, 11½)"/21.5 (25.5, 29)cm from beg. Bind off.

FINISHING
Block pieces to measurements.

Right front band
With A, pick up and k 28 (34, 40) sts along right front edge. Work in St st for 1"/2.5cm. Bind off. Place markers for 5 buttons evenly spaced on band. Work left front band to correspond, working a yo, k2tog buttonhole opposite markers at center of band. Sew shoulder seams. Place markers at 5¼ (5¾, 6¼)"/13.5 (14.5, 16)cm down from shoulders. Sew sleeves to armholes between markers. Sew side and sleeve seams.

Collar
With A, from RS, pick up and k 64 (64, 68) sts evenly around neck edge. Work in seed st inc 1 st each side every other row 6 times—76 (76, 80) sts. Work even until collar measures 2"/5cm. Bind off. Sew on buttons.

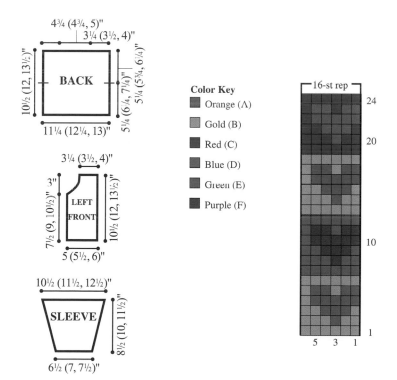

Color Key
- ■ Orange (A)
- ■ Gold (B)
- ■ Red (C)
- ■ Blue (D)
- ■ Green (E)
- ■ Purple (F)

This two-color jacket with hearts and crosses has its roots in basic Swedish motifs. The long stretch of simple dots makes for easy color knitting, and the seed-stitch collar has a ribbed base for even collar turning. Designed by Jean Moss.

SIZES

Instructions are written for size 2. Changes for sizes 3 and 4 are in parentheses.

KNITTED MEASUREMENTS

- Chest (buttoned) 26 (29, 32)"/66 (73.5, 81)cm
- Length 14 (14½, 15½)"/35.5 (37, 39.5)cm
- Upper arm 11½ (11¾, 12½)"/29 (30, 32)cm

MATERIALS

- 5 (6, 6) 1¾oz/50g balls (each approx 123yd/113m) of Rowan Yarns *Wool Cotton* (wool/cotton ③) in #911 red (MC)
- 3 (3, 4) balls in #900 ecru (CC)
- One pair each sizes 3 and 6 (3 and 4mm) needles *or size to obtain gauge*
- Six ½"/13mm buttons

GAUGES

- 24 sts and 28 rows to 4"/10cm over St st foll chart rows 10-17 using larger needles.
- 24 sts and 24 rows to 4"/10cm over Fair Isle pat using larger needles.
Take time to check gauges.

Note When changing colors, twist yarn on WS to prevent holes in work.

SEED STITCH

(over an odd number of sts)
Row 1 K1, *p1, k1; rep from * to end.
Row 2 K the purl and p the knit sts.
Rep row 2 for seed st.

BACK

With smaller needles and MC, cast on 79 (85, 95) sts. Work in k1, p1 rib for 9 rows. K next row on WS, inc 1 st in first st—80 (86, 96) sts. Change to larger needles.

Beg chart pat
Row 1 (RS) Work last 4 (7, 0) sts of chart, work 24-st rep 2 (3, 4) times, work first 4 (7, 0) sts of chart. Cont in pat as established through row 17, then rep rows 10-17 only until piece measures 8 (8¼, 8¾)"/20.5 (21, 22)cm from beg.

Armhole shaping
Beg with row 21, work through row 50 of chart, then rep rows 48-50 to end of piece and AT SAME TIME, shape armhole by binding off 4 (5, 6) sts at beg of next 2 rows, dec 1 st each side every other row 5 (6, 9) times—62 (64, 66) sts. Work even until armhole measures 5½ (5¾, 6¼)"/14 (14.5, 16)cm.

Neck and shoulder shaping
Next row (RS) Place center 26 (26, 28) sts on a holder and AT SAME TIME dec 1 st from each neck edge on next row, and bind off 8 (9, 9) sts from each shoulder edge once, 9 sts once.

LEFT FRONT

With smaller needles and MC, cast on 39 (43, 47) sts. Work in k1, p1 rib for 9 rows. K next row on WS, inc 1 (0, 1) st in first st—40 (43, 48) sts. Change to larger needles.

Beg chart pat

Row 1 (RS) Work last 4 (7, 0) sts of chart, work 24-st rep 1 (1, 2) times, work first 12 (12, 0) sts. Cont in pat as established through row 17, then rep rows 10-17 only until piece measures 8 (8¼, 8¾)"/20.5 (21, 22)cm from beg.

Armhole shaping

Beg with row 21, work through row 50 of chart, then rep rows 48-50 to end of piece and AT SAME TIME, shape armhole by binding off 4 (5, 6) sts from armhole edge (beg of RS rows) once, dec 1 st every other row 5 (6, 9) times—31 (32, 33) sts. Work even until armhole measures 3½ (3¾, 4¼)"/9 (9.5, 11)cm, end with a RS row.

Neck and shoulder shaping

Next row (WS) Bind off 4 (4, 5) sts, work to end. Cont to dec 1 st from neck edge *every* row 10 times and AT SAME TIME, when same length as back, bind off 8 (9, 9) sts from shoulder edge once and 9 sts once.

Work to correspond to left front, reversing all shaping and working chart pat as foll:

Row 1 (RS) Work last 12 (12, 0) sts of chart, work 24-st rep 1 (1, 2) times, work first 4 (7, 0) sts.

SLEEVES

With smaller needles and MC, cast on 35 (37, 41) sts. Work in seed st for 8 rows, inc 1 st on last row—36 (38, 42) sts. Change to larger needles.

Beg chart pat

Row 1 (RS) Work last 6 (7, 9) sts of chart, work 24-st rep once, work first 6 (7, 9) sts of chart. Cont in pat as established, working through row 17, then rep rows 10-17 and AT SAME TIME, inc 1 st each side every alternate 2nd and 4th rows a total of 16 (10, 6) times, then every 4th row 0 (6, 11) times—68 (70, 76) sts. Work even until piece measures 8½ (9½, 10½)"/21.5 (24, 26.5)cm from beg.

Cap shaping

Bind off 4 (5, 6) sts at beg of next 2 rows. Dec 1 st each side every other row 5 (6, 9) times—50 (48, 46) sts. Bind off.

Block pieces to measurements. Sew shoulder seams. Sew sleeves into armholes. Sew side and sleeve seams.

Buttonband

With smaller needles and MC, cast on 5 sts. Work in seed st, sewing band to left front and stretching slightly while knitting, and cont until band fits to neck shaping. Bind off. Place markers for 6 buttons on band, the first and last at ¼"/.5cm from outer edges and the others spaced evenly between.

Buttonhole band

Work as for buttonband, working buttonholes opposite markers as foll:

Buttonhole row (RS) Work 2 sts, bind off 2 sts, work to end. On next row, cast on 2 sts over bound-off sts.

COLLAR

With smaller needles and MC, beg at 2 sts inside of right front band, pick up and k 26 (26, 27) sts along right front neck, 33 (33, 35) sts from back neck, other side to correspond—85 (85, 89) sts. **Row 1 (WS)** *K1, p1; rep from * to last st, k1. **Row 2** *P1, k1; rep from * to last st, p1. Rep last 2 rows once more. **Next row (WS)** K1, inc 1 st in next st, then beg with p1, work seed st to last 2 sts, inc 1 st in next st, k1. **Next row** P1, work seed st to last st, p1. Rep these 2 rows until collar measures 2 (2, 2¼)"/5 (5, 5.5)cm from beg of seed st. Bind off in pat. Sew on buttons.

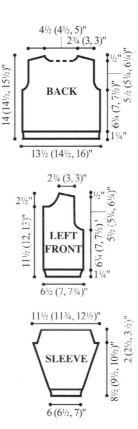

BACK

4½ (4½, 5)"
2¾ (3, 3)"
½"
14 (14½, 15½)"
6¾ (7, 7½)"
5½ (5¾, 6¼)"
1¼"
13½ (14½, 16)"

LEFT FRONT

2¾ (3, 3)"
2½"
½"
11½ (12, 13)"
6¾ (7, 7½)"
5½ (5¾, 6¼)"
1¼"
6½ (7, 7¼)"

SLEEVE

11½ (11¾, 12½)"
8½ (9½, 10½)"
2 (2½, 3½)"
6 (6½, 7)"

Color Key

■ Red (MC)

☐ Ecru (CC)

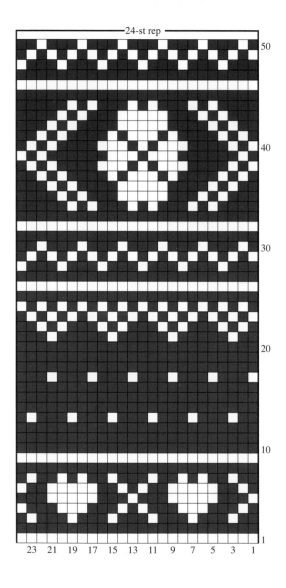

MULTI-STRIPED PULLOVER
Zippity doo dah

Random color picks let you create your own style and personality while knitting this lightweight wool pullover. A garter-stitch edging and a set-in neck zipper complete the look. Designed by Veronica Manno.

SIZES

Instructions are written for size 2. Changes for sizes 3 and 4 are in parentheses.

KNITTED MEASUREMENTS

- Chest 24 (26, 28)"/61 (66, 71)cm
- Length 13½ (14½, 15½)"/34 (37, 39.5)cm
- Upper arm 10 (11, 12)"/25 (28, 30)cm

MATERIALS

- 1 1¾oz/50g hank (each approx 175yd/161m) of Koigu Wool Designs *Premium Merino* (wool ②) each in #2174 dk blue (A), #2229 red (B), #2260 purple (C), #2180 yellow (D), #2343 lt green (E), #2300 lt blue (F), #2390 brown (G), #2231 lt pink (H), #2403 grey (I), #2210 orange (J) and #2188 gold (K)
- One pair size 3 (3mm) needles *or size to obtain gauge*
- One 5"/125mm blue neck zipper
- Size 3 (3mm) circular needle, 16"/40cm long

GAUGE

26 sts and 40 rows to 4"/10cm over St st using size 3 (3mm) needles.
Take time to check gauge.

STRIPE PATTERN

Working in varied colors as desired, work 2 rows of each color.

BACK

With A, cast on 78 (84, 92) sts. K 5 rows. Then cont in St st and stripe pat until piece measures 13½ (14½, 15½)"/34 (37, 39.5)cm from beg. Bind off.

FRONT

Work as for back until piece measures 9 (10, 11)"/23 (25.5, 28)cm from beg.

Neck opening
Next row (RS) K37 (40, 44), join another ball of yarn and bind off center 4 sts, work to end. Work both sides at once for 3"/7.5cm more.

Neck shaping
Bind off 3 (4, 5) sts from each neck edge on next row once, then bind off 3 sts from each neck edge every other row twice, 2 sts once. When same length as back, bind off 26 (28, 31) sts each side for shoulders.

SLEEVES

With A, cast on 46 (48, 52) sts. K 5 rows. Then cont in St st and stripe pat, inc 1 st each side every 8th row 10 (12, 13) times—66 (72, 78) sts. Work even until piece measures 9 (10, 11)"/23 (25.5, 28)cm from beg. Bind off.

FINISHING

Block pieces to measurements. With A, pick up and k 26 sts along one placket edge and work 3 rows in garter st. Bind off. Work other edge in same way. Sew shoulder seams. With A, pick up and k 66 (70, 74) sts evenly around neck edge. Work in garter st for 5 rows. Bind off. Sew in zipper under opening. Place markers at 5 (5½, 6)"/12.5 (14, 15)cm down from shoulders. Sew sleeves to armholes between markers. Sew side and sleeve seams.

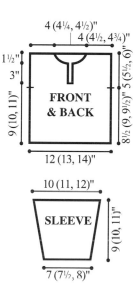

4 (4¼, 4½)"

4 (4½, 4¾)"

1½"

3"

9 (10, 11)"

FRONT & BACK

8½ (9, 9½)" 5 (5½, 6)"

12 (13, 14)"

10 (11, 12)"

SLEEVE

9 (10, 11)"

7 (7½, 8)"

Bouquets of flowers in striped vases are repeated throughout this whimsical childs' cardigan. Two-color ribbing and picot edges provide the trim for this design by Kaffe Fassett.

SIZES
Instructions are written for size 2. Changes for size 4 are in parentheses.

KNITTED MEASUREMENTS
Chest 24 (28)"/61 (71)cm
Length 10¾ (11½)"/27 (29)cm
Upper arm 11¼ (12½)"/28.5 (32)cm

MATERIALS
3 (3) 1¾oz/50g balls (each approx 186yd/170m) of Rowan/Westminster *Fiber 4-Ply Cotton* (cotton ②) in #117 brick red (MC)
1 ball each in #108 blue (A), #106 magenta (B), #105 orange (C), #112 ecru (D), #109 green (E), #118 celery (F) and #120 lt pink (G)
Sizes 3 and 4 (3.25 and 3.5mm) needles *or size to obtain gauge*
Bobbins
Six ½"/13mm buttons

GAUGE
28 sts and 36 rows to 4"/10cm over St st foll chart using larger needles.
Take time to check gauge.

Note Each vase motif is worked with separate strands of yarn. Wind MC onto bobbins to work spaces between motifs. Do not carry colors across back of work.

BODY
With smaller needles and A, cast on 150 (170) sts. Work in St st for 4 rows.
Eyelet turning row (RS) K1, *yo, k2tog; rep from *, end k1. P 1 row.
Beg 2-color rib
Next row (RS) *K2 with B, p2 with C; rep from *, end k2 with B. **Next row** *P2 with B, k2 with C; rep from *, end p2 with B. Rep these 2 rows 3 times more. Change to larger needles and k next row with MC, inc 19 (23) sts evenly spaced—169 (193) sts. Work 3 more rows with MC.
Beg chart pat
Row 5 (RS) Work 24-st rep 7 (8) times, end k1 with MC. Cont to foll chart in this way, rep rows 1-68 until row 38 (42) is completed.
Separate for fronts and back
Next row (RS) Work 38 (44) sts and place on holder for right front, bind off 8 sts, work until there are 77 (89) sts for back, leave rem sts unworked. Cont to work back sts only until armhole measures 5 (5½)"/12.5 (14)cm.
Neck and shoulder shaping
Bind off 7 (9) sts at beg of next 4 rows, 8 (10) sts at beg of next 2 rows and AT SAME TIME, bind off center 25 sts and working both sides at once, bind off 4 sts from back neck edge once.

RIGHT FRONT

Return to 38 (44) sts on right front and work even until armhole measures 3½ (4)"/9 (10)cm.

Neck shaping

Next row (RS) Bind off 4 sts, work to end. Cont to shape neck, binding off 3 sts from neck edge twice, 2 sts 3 times—22 (28 sts). When armhole measures 5 (5½)"/12.5 (14)cm, bind off 7 (9) sts from armhole edge twice and 8 (10) sts once.

LEFT FRONT

Join yarn to rem sts and bind off 8 sts for armhole, work to end. Cont as for right front, reversing shaping.

SLEEVES

With smaller needles and A, cast on 42 (46) sts. Work edge and rib as for body. Change to larger needles and k next row with MC, inc 13 sts evenly spaced—55 (59) sts. Work 3 rows more with MC.

Beg chart pat

Row 5 (RS) Inc 1 st in first st, beg with st 11 (9) of chart row 5, work 24-st rep across, ending with inc 1 st in last st. Cont to inc 1 st each side (working inc sts into chart pat) every 4th row 11 (13) times more—79 (87) sts. Work even until piece measures 8 (9)"/20.5 (23)cm above turning ridge. Bind off.

FINISHING

Block pieces to measurements. Turn up hems to WS and sew in place. Sew sleeves into armholes, beg and end at center of bound-off sts. Sew sleeve seams.

Buttonband

With smaller needles and MC, pick up and k 66 (70) sts evenly along right front edge. Change to B and C and work in 2-color rib for 4 rows. Change to A and p 1 row. Work eyelet turning row. Work 4 more rows in St st. Bind off. Place markers for 6 buttons evenly spaced on band. Work buttonhole band to correspond, working 6 buttonholes by binding off 2 sts for each buttonhole on row 3 and casting on 2 sts over each buttonhole on row 4.

COLLAR

With smaller needles and MC, pick up and k 102 sts evenly around neck edge excluding front bands. Change to B and C and work in 2-color rib for 1¼"/3cm. Then work eyelet row and facing with A as before. Bind off. Fold edges along eyelet rows and sew to WS. Sew on buttons.

Color Key

- ■ Brick red (MC)
- ■ Blue (A)
- □ Ecru (D)
- ■ Green (E)
- □ Celery (F)
- □ Lt pink (G)

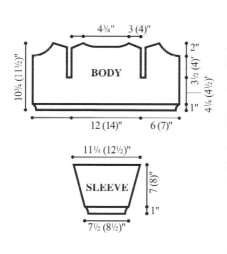

4³⁄₄" · 3 (4)"

10³⁄₄ (11¹⁄₂)"

BODY

2"

3¹⁄₂ (4)"

4¹⁄₄ (4¹⁄₂)"

1"

12 (14)" · 6 (7)"

11¹⁄₄ (12¹⁄₂)"

SLEEVE

7 (8)"

1"

7¹⁄₂ (8¹⁄₂)"

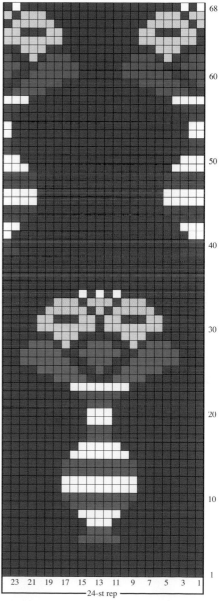

68

60

50

40

30

20

10

1

23 21 19 17 15 13 11 9 7 5 3 1

24-st rep

For Intermediate Knitters

This quick-to-knit chair cover is a perfect way to liven up your toddler's room. Just adjust the width and length to accommodate any size chair. Designed by Jean Guirguis.

KNITTED MEASUREMENTS

■ Approx 13"/33cm wide x 20"50.5cm long

MATERIALS

■ 5 1¾oz/50g balls (each approx 90yd/83m) Berroco, Inc. *Plush* (nylon ⑤) in #1934 black (MC),

■ 3 balls in #1901 cream (CC)

■ One pair size 9 (5.5mm) needles *or size to obtain gauge*

■ 1½yd/1.5m satin ribbon, ⅞"/2cm wide

GAUGE

15 sts and 24 rows to 4"/10cm over St st using size 9 (5.5mm) needles. *Take time to check gauge.*

COVER

With MC, cast on 60 sts. Work in St st for 120 rows for back piece. Place marker each side of row. Cont in st st and work 120 rows of chart for front piece. Work in garter st for 2½"/6.5cm for flap. Bind off.

FINISHING

Fold piece so that right sides of front and back piece are facing each other. Sew side seams. Turn right side out. Fold garter st flap to right side of front piece and sew side seams. Turn right side out for overlap. Cut ribbon in two equal lengths and sew to sides about halfway from lower edge.

Color Key

■ Black (MC)

□ Cream (CC)

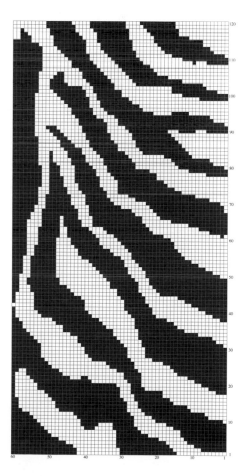

Each section of this colorful cardigan, designed by Kristen Nicholas, is interpreted using a different colorway for sheer fun and variety. Easy rolled and garter-stitch edges keep this style simple.

SIZES

Instructions are written for size 2. Changes for sizes 3 and 4 are in parentheses.

KNITTED MEASUREMENTS

- Chest 26 (28, 30)"/66 (71, 76)cm
- Length 13 (14, 15)"/33 (35.5, 38)cm
- Upper arm 11 (12, 13)"/28 (30, 33)cm

MATERIALS

Version 1

- 2 (2, 3) 1¾oz/50g hanks (each approx 95yd/85m) of Classic Elite Yarns *Tapestry* (wool/mohair ④) each in #2295 blue (A), #2251 gold (B) and #2291 brown (D)
- 3 (3, 4) hanks in #2268 red (C)

Version 2

- 2 (2, 3) hanks each in #2234 raspberry (A), #2231 turquoise (B) and #2272 green (D)
- 3 (3, 4) hanks in #2284 orange (C)
- One each sizes 5 and 7 (3.75 and 4.5mm) circular needle, 24"/60cm long
- Five ¾"/20mm buttons

GAUGE

22 sts and 26 rows to 4"/10cm over color pat foll charts using larger needles.
Take time to check gauge.

Notes 1 Sweater is worked in 2-color version foll charts. **2** Body is worked in one piece to armhole, then both fronts and back are worked separately to shoulder. **3** When changing colors, twist yarns on WS to prevent holes in work.

SEED STITCH PATTERN

(over an odd number of sts)
Row 1 (RS) K1, *p1, k1; rep from * to end.
Row 2 K the purl and p the knit sts.
Rep row 2 for seed st pat.

BODY

With smaller needles and A, cast on 129 (139, 149) sts. Work in St st for 4 rows. Work 2 rows in seed st, inc 15 (17, 17) sts evenly on 2nd row—144 (156, 166) sts. Change to larger needles.
Beg lower body chart pat
Row 1 (RS) Beg with st 9 (8, 8) of lower body chart, work to end of chart, then work 10-st rep 14 (15, 16) times, end with st 2 (3, 3). Cont in pat as established until piece measures 4 (4¼, 4¾)"/10 (11, 12)cm from beg, end with a WS row. With A, k 2 rows, p 1 row (for ridge).
Beg upper body chart pat
Row 1 (RS) Beg with st 19 (13, 18) of upper body chart, work to end of chart, then work 20-st rep 7 (7, 8) times, end with st 2 (8, 3). Cont in pat as established until piece measures 7½ (8, 8½)"/19 (20.5, 21.5)cm from beg, end with a WS row.

Divide for fronts and back

Next row (RS) Work 36 (39, 41) sts for right front, join another 2 balls of yarn and work 72 (78, 84) sts for back, join another 2 balls of yarn and work rem 36 (39, 41) sts for left front. Work each side separately until a total of 11 (12, 13)"/28 (30.5, 33)cm from beg.

Front neck shaping

Cont to work back even, AT SAME TIME, bind off from each front neck edge 10 (11, 12) sts once, dec 1 st at each neck edge every other row 4 times—22 (24, 25) sts for each front shoulder. Work even until pieces measure 13 (14, 15)"/33 (35.5, 38)cm from beg. Bind off sts on all pieces.

Note Make one sleeve foll sleeve A chart, one sleeve foll sleeve B chart. With smaller needles and A, cast on 27 (29, 31) sts. Work in St st for 4 rows. Work 2 rows in seed st, inc 5 (5, 7) sts evenly on 2nd row—32 (34, 38) sts. Change to larger needles.

Beg sleeve chart

Row 1 (RS) Beg with st 10 (9, 7) of sleeve A (or B) chart, work to end of chart, then work 10-st rep 3 times, end with st 1 (2, 4). Cont in pat as established, inc 1 st each side (working inc sts into chart pat) every 4th row 14 (16, 17) times—60 (66, 72) sts. Work even until piece measures 9½ (11, 12)"/24 (28, 30.5)cm above rolled edge. Bind off.

FINISHING

Block pieces to measurements. Sew shoulder seams. Sew sleeves into armholes. Sew sleeve seams.

Neckband

With smaller needles and A, pick up and k 72 (79, 84) sts evenly around neck edge. K 5 rows. Bind off.

Left front band

With smaller needles and A (omitting lower edge), pick up and k 61 (65, 69) sts along left front edge. K 5 rows. Bind off.

Right front band

Work as for left front band for 3 rows. **Buttonhole row (RS)** K3, * bind off 3 sts, k10 (11, 12); rep from * 3 times more, bind off 3 sts, k3. **Next row** Knit, casting on 2 sts over each 3-st buttonhole. Bind off all sts. Sew on buttons.

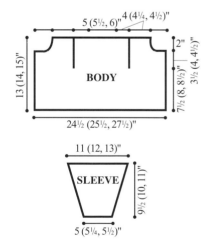

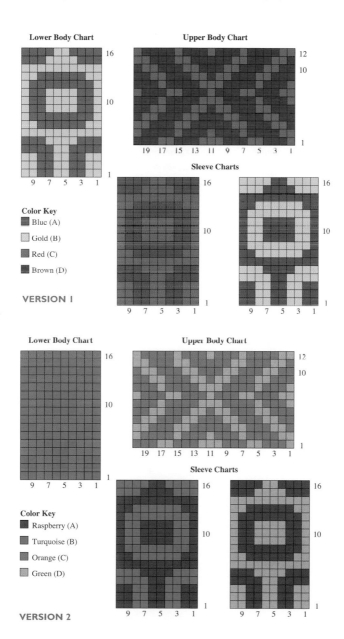

Lower Body Chart

16

10

1

9 7 5 3 1

Upper Body Chart

12

10

1

19 17 15 13 11 9 7 5 3 1

Color Key

■ Blue (A)

□ Gold (B)

■ Red (C)

■ Brown (D)

VERSION 1

Sleeve Charts

16

10

1

9 7 5 3 1

16

10

1

9 7 5 3 1

Lower Body Chart

16

10

1

9 7 5 3 1

Upper Body Chart

12

10

1

19 17 15 13 11 9 7 5 3 1

Color Key

■ Raspberry (A)

■ Turquoise (B)

■ Orange (C)

□ Green (D)

VERSION 2

Sleeve Charts

16

10

1

9 7 5 3 1

16

10

1

9 7 5 3 1

Bobbles are the focal point of all the patterns in this charming tunic-length pullover with eyelet point trims and buttoned shoulder closure. Designed by Kirstin Cowan.

SIZES

Instructions are written for size 2. Changes for sizes 3 and 4 are in parentheses.

KNITTED MEASUREMENTS

- Chest 25 (29½, 34)"/63.5 (75, 86)cm
- Length 15 (16, 17)"/38 (40.5, 43)cm
- Upper arm 10 (11, 12)"/25.5 (28, 30)cm

MATERIALS

- 4 (5, 6) 1¾oz/50g balls (each approx 135yd/124m) of Patons® *Country Garden DK* (wool ③) in #41 lt green
- One pair size 6 (4mm) needles *or size to obtain gauge*
- Two ½"/13mm buttons

GAUGE

25 sts and 30 rows to 4"/10cm across all pat sts using size 6 (4mm) needles.
Take time to check gauge.

STITCH GLOSSARY

MB
Make bobble by k1, p1, k1, p1 all in one st. Turn, p4. Turn, k4. Turn, p4. Turn, k2tog twice, then with LH needle, sl first st over 2nd st on RH needle.

Double dec
Insert RH needle into next 2 sts as for a k2tog, sl to RH needle, k1, pass 2 slipped sts over the k st.

LT
Left twist Wyib, skip first st and k 2nd st tbl, then k first st through front loop (tfl) and slip both sts off needle tog.

RT
Right twist Wyib, skip first st and k 2nd st tfl, then k first st tfl and slip both sts off needle tog.

5-st cable
Drop first sl st and hold to *front*, sl next 3 sts to RH needle, drop 2nd sl st and hold to *front*, pick up first dropped st with LH needle, sl 3 sts from RH needle back to LH needle, pick up 2nd dropped st with LH needle, k5.

BERRY VINE PANEL

Over 15 sts
Row 1 and all WS row Purl.
Row 2 (RS) K6, RT, k1, LT, k4.
Row 4 K5, RT, k3, LT, k3.
Row 6 K4, RT, k5, LT, k2.
Row 8 K3, RT, k1, LT, k4, MB, k2.
Row 10 K2, RT, k3, LT, k6.
Row 12 K2, MB, k5, LT, k5.
Rep rows 1-12 for berry vine panel.

DOUBLE CABLE PANEL

(over 16 sts)
Rows 1, 3, 7 and 9 (WS) [K2, p1, k3, p1] twice, k2.

Rows 2 and 8 [P2, k1, p3, k1] twice, p2.
Row 4 P2, sl 1 wyib, p3, sl 1 wyib, p2, k1, p3, k1, p2.
Row 5 K2, p1, k3, p1, k2, sl 1 wyif, k3, sl 1 wyif, k2.
Row 6 P2, work 5-st cable, p2, k1, p1, MB, p1, k1, p2.
Row 10 P2, k1, p3, k1, p2, sl 1 wyib, p3, sl 1 wyib, p2.
Row 11 K2, sl 1 wyif, k3, sl 1 wyif, k2, p1, k3, p1, k2.
Row 12 P2, k1, p1, MB, p1, k1, p2, work 5-st cable, p2.
Rep rows 1-12 for double cable panel.

SINGLE CABLE PANEL
(over 7 sts)
Note This panel is not required for size 2.
Rows 1, 3, 7, 9 and 11 (WS) K2, p1, k3, p1.
Rows 2, 8 and 10 K1, p3, k1, p2.
Row 4 Sl 1 wyib, p3, sl 1 wyib, p2.
Row 5 K2, sl 1 wyif, k3, sl 1 wyif.
Row 6 Work 5-st cable, p2.
Row 12 K1, p1, MB, p1, k1, p2.
Rep rows 1-12 for single cable panel.
Note When measuring length of pieces, measure to ends of scallop points, excluding bobbles.

BACK
Cast on 71 (85, 99) sts and work scallop edge as foll:
Row 1 (RS) P7*, *MB, p13; rep from * to last 8 sts, MB, p7.
Row 2 and all WS rows: Purl.
Row 3 K1, *yo, p5, double dec, p5, yo, k1; rep from * to end.

Row 5 K2, *yo, p4, double dec, p4, yo, k3; rep from * to last 13 sts, yo, p4, double dec, p4, yo, k2.
Row 7 K3, *yo, p3, double dec, p3, yo, k5; rep from * to last 12 sts, yo, p3, double dec, p3, yo, k3.
Row 9 K4, *yo, p2, double dec, p2, yo, k7; rep from * to last 11 sts, yo, p2, double dec, p2, yo, k4.
Row 11 K5, *yo, p1, double dec, p1, yo, k9; rep from * to last 10 sts, yo, p1, double dec, p1, yo, k5.
Row 13 K6, *yo, double dec, yo, k11; rep from * to last 9 sts, yo, double dec, yo, k6.
Row 14 Purl.
Next row (RS) Purl, inc 7 sts purlwise evenly across—78 (92, 106) sts.
Size 2
Beg pat—Next row (WS) [Work 16-st double cable panel, 15-st berry panel] twice, work 16-st double cable pat.
Size 3
Beg pat—Next row (WS) Work 7-st single cable panel, work 16-st double cable panel, [15-st berry panel, 16-st double cable panel] twice, 7-st single cable panel.
Size 4
Beg pat—Next row (WS) Work 7-st single cable panel, 16-st double cable panel, 7-st single cable panel, 15-st berry panel, 14-st double cable panel, 15-st berry panel, 7-st single cable panel, 16-st double cable panel, 7-st single cable panel. Cont in this way until piece measures 10 (10½, 11)"/25.5 (26.5, 28) cm from scallop point.
Armhole shaping
Bind off 7 sts at beg of next 2 rows—64 (78,

92) sts. Work even until armhole measures 5 (5½, 6)"/12.5 (14, 15)cm. Bind off.

FRONT

Work as for back until armhole measures 3 (3½, 4)"/7.5 (9, 10)cm.

Neck shaping

Next row (RS) Work 24 (31, 38) sts, join a 2nd ball of yarn and bind off center 16 sts, work to end. Working both sides at once, bind off 2 sts from each neck edge once, dec 1 st *every* row 4 (5, 6) times— 18 (24, 30) sts each side. When same length as back, bind off sts each side.

SLEEVES

Cast on 43 (43, 57) sts and work 14-row scallop edge as on back. **Next row (RS)** Purl, inc 4 sts evenly across—47 (47, 61) sts. **Beg pat—Next row (WS)** Work 16-st double cable panel, 7-st single cable panel 0 (0, 1) time, 15-st berry panel, 16-st double cable panel, 7-st single cable panel 0 (0, 1) time. Work pats as established inc 1 st each side (working incs in reverse St st) every 6th (6th, 8th) row 9 (12, 8) times—65 (71, 77) sts. Work even until piece measures 9½ (10, 10½)"/24 (25.5, 26.5)cm from beg. Bind off.

FINISHING

Block pieces to measurements. Sew right shoulder seam.

Neckband

With smaller needles, pick up and k 66 (72, 78) sts around neck edge. Work 5 rows in garter st. **Next row (RS)** K3, *MB, k5; rep from * to last 9 sts, MB, k8. Bind off.

Shoulder placket

Pick up and k 21 sts along left front shoulder and neckband. K 2 rows. **Next row (WS)** K2, k2tog, yo, k6. K2tog, yo, k to end. K 2 rows. Bind off. Sew buttons on back shoulder to correspond to buttonholes and button closed. Place markers at 5 (5½, 6)"/13 (14, 15)cm down from shoulders. Sew sleeves to armholes between markers. Sew side and sleeve seams.

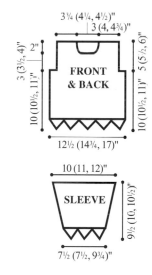

3¼ (4¼, 4½)"
3 (4, 4¾)"
3 (3½, 4)"
2"
10 (10½, 11)"
5 (5½, 6)"
FRONT & BACK
10 (10½, 11)"
12½ (14¾, 17)"

10 (11, 12)"
SLEEVE
9½ (10, 10½)"
7½ (7½, 9¾)"

An all-over basketweave pattern stitch gives style and definition to this girl's cotton 3-piece set. Crocheted flowers are sewn on with smaller flower buttons for centers. Designed by Nicky Epstein.

SIZES

Instructions are written for size 2. Changes for size 4 are in parentheses.

KNITTED MEASUREMENTS

Jacket
- Chest 22 (25)"/56 (63.5)cm
- Length 13 (15)"/33 (38)cm
- Upper arm 9 (10)"/23 (25.5)cm

Pants
- Hip 18 (22)"/45.5 (56)cm
- Length 11 (13¾)"/28 (35)cm

Hat
- Circumference 15 (17)"/38 (43)cm

MATERIALS

- 11 (12) 1¾oz/50g balls (each approx 173yd/160m) of Naturally/S.R. Kertzer, Ltd. *Magic Garden Cotton Candy DK* (wool/cotton ③) in #508 mango (MC)
- 1 ball each in #507 lime (A), #502 pink (B) and #509 yellow (C)
- One pair size 3 (3mm) needles *or size to obtain gauge*
- Size 3 (3mm) circular needle, 24"/60cm long
- 3 small buttons
- ¾ yd/.70m of ¾"/2cm elastic
- Stitch holders

GAUGE

24 sts and 38 rows to 4"/10cm over basketweave pat st using size 3 (3mm) needles. *Take time to check gauge.*

BASKETWEAVE PATTERN STITCH

(multiple of 10 sts plus 5)
Rows 1, 3 and 5 (RS) K5, *p5, k5; rep from * to end.
Rows 2 and 4 Purl.
Rows 6, 8 and 10 K5, *p5, k5; rep from * to end.
Rows 7 and 9 Knit.
Rep rows 1-10 for basketweave pat st.

JACKET

BACK

With MC, cast on 77 (87) sts. K 4 rows. Keeping a k1 selvage st each side, work in basketweave pat st, dec 1 st each side every 12th (14th) row 5 times—67 (77) sts. Work even until piece measures 8½ (10)"/21.5 (25.5)cm from beg.

Armhole shaping
Bind off 5 sts at beg of next 2 rows—57 (67) sts. Work even until armhole measures 4½ (5)"/11.5 (12.5)cm. Bind off all sts.

LEFT FRONT

With MC, cast on 42 (47) sts. K 4 rows. Keeping a k1 selvage st at each side, work in basketweave pat st, dec 1 at armhole edge (beg of RS rows) every 12th (14th) row 5 times—37 (42) sts. Work even until piece measures 8½ (10)"/21.5 (25.5)cm from beg.

Armhole shaping

Bind off 5 sts from armhole edge on next RS row—32 (37) sts. Work even until armhole measures 3 (3½)"/7.5 (9)cm.

Neck shaping

Next row (WS) Bind off 6 sts, work to end. Cont to bind off from neck edge 2 sts 5 times—16 (21) sts. Work even until same length as back. Bind off sts for shoulder.

RIGHT FRONT

Work to correspond to left front, reversing shaping.

SLEEVES

With MC, cast on 42 sts. K 4 rows. Keeping a k1 selvage st each side, work in basketweave pat st, inc 1 st each side every 8th row 7 (10) times—56 (62) sts. Work even until piece measures 9½ (11½)"/24 (29)cm from beg. Bind off.

Flowers

(make 1 each A, B and C)
Cast on 55 sts.

Rows 1, 3 and 5 (WS) purl.

Row 2 (RS) K1, *yo, k2, ssk, k2tog, k2, yo, k1; rep from * to end.

Row 6 *K1, k2tog; rep from *, end k1—37 sts.

Row 7 [P2tog] 18 times, p1—19 sts.

Row 8 [K2tog] 9 times, k1. Pull yarn through rem 10 sts and draw up tightly to fasten. Sew seam of flower.

FINISHING

Block pieces to measurements. Sew shoulder seams. Sew sleeves into armholes. Sew side and sleeve seams.

Pocket trims

With MC, cast on 20 sts. K 6 rows. Sew pocket trims to fronts at 2"/5cm from side seam and 3 (4)"/7.5 (10)cm from lower edge.

Collar

With WS facing and MC, pick up and k 77 sts evenly around collar edge. K 1 row. Keeping a k1 selvage st each side, work in basket weave pat st for 4"/10cm. Place sts on a holder.

Front bands

With MC, pick up and k 72 (84) sts along left front edge. K 4 rows. Bind off. Work right front edge in same way.

Collar trim

With MC and circular needle, pick up and k 19 sts along side of collar, 77 collar sts and 19 sts along other side of collar—115 sts. K 1 row.

Next row (RS) K19, cast on 1 st, k77, cast on 1 st, k19—117 sts. K 1 row. Bind off. Sew trim to front bands. Sew on 3 flowers with a contrast button at each flower center. Sew on snaps under to snap closed.

PANTS

Left leg

With MC, beg at waist edge, cast on 58 (68) sts. Work in k2, p2 rib for 1"/2.5cm. K 2 rows. Work in rib for 1"/2.5cm more, dec 1 st on last row—57 (67) sts. Keeping a k1 selvage st each side, work in basketweave pat for 4 (5¼)"/10 (13.5)cm.

Crotch shaping
Cast on 1 st at beg of next 2 rows, 2 sts at beg of next 4 rows—67 (77) sts. Dec 1 st each side every other row 3 (5) times every 8th row 4 times 53 (59) sts. Work even until leg measures 5½ (7)"/14 (18)cm. K 4 rows. Bind off.

RIGHT LEG
Work to correspond to left leg, reversing shaping.

FINISHING
Block pieces to measurements. Sew legs tog along crotch and leg seams. Fold waistband in half to WS over elastic, cut to fit waist, and sew in place.

HAT
With MC, cast on 87 (97) sts. K 6 rows. Keeping a k1 selvage at each side, work in basketweave pat until piece meaures 5½ (6½)"/14 (16.5)cm from beg. **Next row (RS)** K1, *k2tog; rep from * to end—44 (49) sts. **Next row** P0 (1), *p2tog; rep from * to end—22 (25) sts. K 14 rows (for garter st knot). Bind off.

FINISHING
Block hat flat. sew back seam and draw yarn through tightly at base of garter st knot to gather. Sew knot seam.

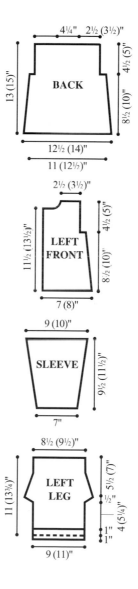

An assortment of colorful argyle diamonds give regimental flair to this bulky toddler cardigan. Designed by Kellie Overbey, the body is knit all in one piece for speedy finishing.

SIZES

Instructions are written for size 2. Changes for size 4 are in parentheses.

KNITTED MEASUREMENTS

- Chest (buttoned) 24 (27)"/61 (68.5)cm
- Length 10 (12¼)"/25.5 (31)cm
- Upper arm 9 (10)"/23 (25.5)cm

MATERIALS

- 2 (2) 3½oz/100g balls (each approx 200yd/180m) of Plymouth Yarns *Encore Worsted* (wool/acrylic ④) in #1204 brown (MC)
- 1 ball each in #1382 yellow (B), #1383 orange (C), and #133 blue (D), #1384 purple (E), #54 green (F), #9601 red (G)
- 1 pair each sizes 5 and 6 (3.75 and 4mm) needles *or size to obtain gauge*
- Stitch markers
- Nine ½"/13mm buttons

GAUGE

20 sts and 25 rows to 4"/10cm over St st and argyle pat foll chart using larger needles. *Take time to check gauge.*

Notes I Use the 16-st and 29-row argyle chart for argyle pat only. Foll schematic diagrams for color placement of diamonds. **2** If desired, the cross lines in red may be worked in duplicate st, foll chart for placement, after pieces are knit. **3** When changing color, twist yarns on WS to prevent holes in work.

BODY

With smaller needles and MC, cast on 114 (130) sts. **Row I (RS)** K2, *p2, p2; rep from * to end. Cont in k2, p2 rib as established for 8 rows, inc 1 st at center of 8th row—115 (131) sts. Change to larger needles.

Beg chart pat

Row I (RS) Foll schematic for color placement for desired size, work 2 sts MC, work 16-st rep 7 (8) times, work 1 st MC. Cont in pat as established until 26 (36) rows of chart have been completed and piece measures 5 (6¾)"/12.5 (17)cm from beg.

Divide for Fronts and Back

Row 27 (37) (RS) Work 26 (30) sts and place on a holder for right front, bind off 4 sts, work until there are 55 (63) sts for back, place rem sts on a holder for left front.

BACK

Working on back sts only, dec 1 st from each armhole edge every other row twice—51 (59) sts. Work even until armhole measures 5 (5½)"/12.5 (14)cm, ending with 4th (5th) complete rep of argyle pat. Bind off all sts.

RIGHT FRONT

Rejoin yarn to work right front sts and dec 1 st from armhole edge every other row twice—24 (28) sts. Work even until armhole measures 3½ (4)"/9 (10)cm.

Neck shaping

Next row (RS) Bind off 6 sts, work to end. Cont to bind off from neck edge 2 sts 3 times—12 (16) sts. When same number of rows as back, bind off rem sts for shoulders.

LEFT FRONT

Rejoin yarn to armhole to work left front and bind off 4 sts, work to end. Complete to correspond to right front, reversing shaping.

SLEEVES

With smaller needles and MC, cast on 34 sts. Work in k2, p2 rib for 8 rows, inc 1 st at center of 8th row—35 sts. Change to larger needles.

Beg chart pat

Row 1 (RS) Foll schematic for color placement for left or right sleeve, work 2 sts with MC, work 16-st rep twice, work 1 st with MC. Cont in pat as established, inc 1 st each side (working inc sts in MC only) on 3rd row then every 8th row 4 (6) times more—45 (49) sts. Work even until piece measures 8½ (10½)"/21.5 (26.5)cm from beg.

Cap shaping

Bind off 2 sts at beg of next 2 rows. Dec 1 st each side every other row 10 times, then *every* row 2 (4) times. Bind off rem 17 sts.

FINISHING

Block pieces to measurements.

Buttonband

With smaller needles and MC, cast on 7 sts. **Row 1 (WS)** K1, *p1, k1; rep from * to end. **Row 2** K2, p1, k1, p1, k2. Rep these 2 rows until piece fits along right front edge, stretching slightly to fit. Place 7 sts on a holder and sew band in place, adjusting length if necessary. Place markers for 8 buttons, the first one in 4th row from lower edge, the last one at 6 rows from top edge and the others spaced evenly between. Work buttonhole band in same way forming buttonholes opposite markers on a RS row as foll: k2, p1, SKP, k2. **Next row (WS)** K1, p1, k1, yo, k1, p1, k1. Sew band to left front. Sew shoulder seams.

Neckband

With smaller needles and MC, pick up and k 65 (69) sts evenly around neck edge. Work in k2, p2 rib for 4 rows. Bind off, forming 1 more buttonhole in 2nd row on buttonhole band. Bind off in rib. Sew sleeves into armholes. Sew sleeve seams. Sew on buttons.

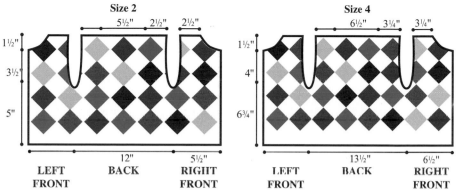

Size 2

5½" 2½" 2½"

1½"

3½"

5"

12" 5½"

LEFT FRONT   BACK   RIGHT FRONT

Size 4

6½" 3¼" 3¼"

1½"

4"

6¾"

13½" 6½"

LEFT FRONT   BACK   RIGHT FRONT

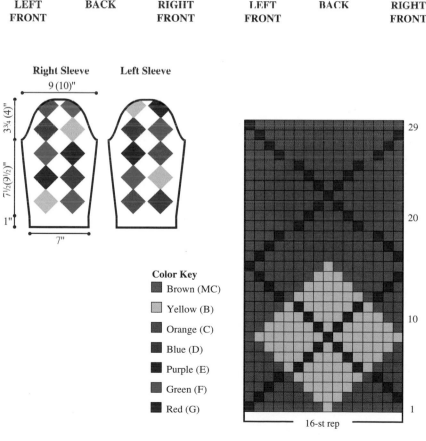

Right Sleeve   **Left Sleeve**

9 (10)"

3¾ (4)"

7½ (9½)"

1"

7"

Color Key

■ Brown (MC)
□ Yellow (B)
■ Orange (C)
■ Blue (D)
■ Purple (E)
■ Green (F)
■ Red (G)

29

20

10

1

16-st rep

This little girl's dress, knit in an all-over lace pattern, has three repeating eyelet patterns, full-fashioned armhole shaping, and turned-up eyelet hems on all edges. Designed by Zabeth Weiner.

SIZES

Instructions are written for size 2. Changes for sizes 3 and 4 are in parentheses.

KNITTED MEASUREMENTS

■ Chest 28 (30, 32)"/71 (76, 81)cm
■ Length 13 (14¼, 14¾)"/33 (36, 37.5)cm

MATERIALS

■ 4 (5, 5) 1¾oz/50g balls (each approx 113yd/105m) of Dale of Norway *Kolibri Cotton* (cotton ③) in #4417 pink
■ One pair size 3 (3mm) knitting needles *or size to obtain gauge*
■ One size 3 (3mm) circular needle, 16"/40cm long
■ One set (4) size 3 (3mm) dpn

GAUGE

22 sts and 32 rows to 4"/10cm over eyelet pat sts foll charts using size 3 (3mm) needles. *Take time to check gauge.*

Note Be sure to have the same number of yo's as decs on each row to keep st count the same. If not, then work these sts in St st instead of yo or dec.

BACK

Cast on 76 (82, 86) sts. Work in St st for 6 rows. **Eyelet row (RS)** K1, *yo, k2tog; rep from *, end k1. Work in St st for 7 rows, inc 1 st on last row—77 (83, 87) sts.

Beg Chart 1

Row 1 (RS) Beg with st 1 (3, 1), work through st 12, then work 10-st rep 6 (7, 7) times, end with st 15, k2 (0, 2). Cont in pat as established through row 12. Work 0 (4, 4) rows in St st.

Beg Chart 2

Row 1 (RS) Beg with st 1, work through st 13, then work 10-st rep 6 (7, 7) times more, end with st 17 (13, 17). Cont in pat as established through row 28. Then rep rows 1-28 once, rows 1-10 (14, 14) once.

Beg Chart 3

Row 1 (RS) K1, work sts 1 (3, 1) through 12 once, then work 10-st rep across, end with st 25 (23, 25), k1. Cont in pat as established through row 11. **Next row (WS)** P12 (10, 12), *k1, p1 tbl, k1, p7; rep from *, end k1, p1 tbl, k1, p12 (10, 12).

Armhole shaping

Cont in pat by k the knit and p the purl sts and k1 tbl the p1 tbl sts, shape armhole by binding off 5 sts at beg of next 2 rows. On next RS row, foll Chart 4 in pat as established (set up with the k1 tbl sts over the double dec in row 11 of chart 3) and AT SAME TIME, work dec as foll: K2, k2tog, work to last 4 sts, SKP, k2. Rep dec row every other row 5 (5, 6) times more—55 (61, 63) sts. Work even until there are 5 (6, 7) 4-row reps of Chart 4.

Neck shaping

Next row (RS) Work 18 (17, 17) sts, join another ball of yarn and bind off center 19 (27, 29) sts, work to end. Cont to work both sides at once, dec 1 st at each neck edge every other row 4 times. K 1 row.

Bind off rem 14 (13, 13) sts each side for shoulders.

FRONT

Work as for back until there are 3 (4, 5) 4-row reps of Chart 4.

Neck shaping

Next row (RS) Work 21 (20, 20) sts, join another ball of yarn and bind off center 13 (21, 23) sts, work to end. Cont to work both sides at once, dec 1 st at each neck edge every other row 7 times—14 (13, 13) sts each side. When same length as back, bind off sts each side for shoulders.

FINISHING

Block pieces to measurements. Sew shoulder and side seams.

Neckband

With circular needle, pick up and k 92 (106, 112) sts evenly around neck edge. Join and work in rnds. K 4 rnds. **Next (eyelet) rnd** *K2tog, yo; rep from * around. K 4 rnds. Bind off.

Armhole bands

With dpn, pick up and k 48 (52, 56) sts evenly around armhole. Work as for neckband. Fold all bands to WS along eyelet ridge and sew in place.

Stitch Key

- P on RS, k on WS
- K on RS, p on WS
- Yo
- Sl 1, k2tog, psso
- K2tog on RS, p2tog on WS
- Ssk on RS, p2tog tbl on WS
- K3tog on RS, p3tog on WS
- Yo twice
- Sl 2, k3tog, p2sso
- K1 tbl on RS, p1 tbl on WS

Chart 1
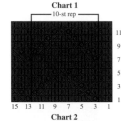

Chart 2

Chart 3
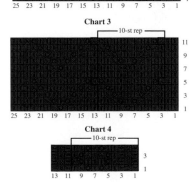

Chart 4

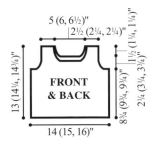

5 (6, 6½)"
2½ (2¼, 2¼)"
(1¼, 1¼)"
1½ (1¼, 3¾)"
13 (14¼, 14¾)"
8¾ (9¾, 9¾)"
2¼ (3¼, 3¾)"

FRONT & BACK

14 (15, 16)"

You've got mail

A geometric cloud background with a picket fence sets the scene for this charming fold-down mailbox pullover. Designed by Betsy Westman.

SIZES

Instructions are written for size 2. Changes for sizes 3 and 4 are in parentheses.

KNITTED MEASUREMENTS

- Chest 27 (28, 29½)"/68.5 (71, 75)cm
- Length 11¾ (12¾, 13½)"/30 (32.5, 34)cm
- Upper arm 11 (12, 13)"/28 (30, 33)cm

MATERIALS

- 2 (2, 2) 1¾oz/50g balls (each approx 146yd/135m) of Sesia/Lane Borgosesia *Cablé 2005* (cotton ③) in #470 blue (A), #87 teal (B) and#425 lt blue (C)
- 1 (1, 1) ball each in #222 lt green (D), #525 dk green (E), #80 ecru (F), #67 black (G), #52 beige (H) and #201 red (I)
- One pair each sizes 3 and 4 (3 and 3.5mm) needles *or size to obtain gauge*
- Size 3 (3mm) circular needle 16"/40cm long
- One ½"/13mm button

GAUGE

26 sts and 33 rows to 4"/10cm over St st foll chart using larger needles.
Take time to check gauge.
Note When changing colors, twist yarns on WS to prevent holes. Do not carry yarn across back of work, but work each segment of color with a separate ball or bobbin.

BACK

With smaller needles and E, cast on 88 (92, 96) sts. Work in St st for 2 rows. Change to larger needles and work chart for back in chosen size through row 95 (102, 109). Bind off.

FRONT

Cast on and work hem as for back, then cont in chart for front through row 42. **Row 43** Work to 12 sts in color F for mailbox flap, bind off these 12 sts (for pocket), work to end. On next row, cast on 12 sts over bound-off sts. Cont to foll chart through row 79 (84, 92).

Neck shaping
On next row, bind off center 18 (20, 22) sts, and cont to work both sides at once, bind off 4 sts from each neck edge once, 3 sts once, dec 1 st *every* row 3 times, dec 1 st every other row 2 (2, 3) times. When same length as back, bind off rem 23 (24, 24) sts each side for shoulders.

SLEEVES

With smaller needles and D, cast on 42 (46, 46) sts. Work in St st for 3 rows. Change to larger needles and work chart for sleeves, inc 1 st each side every 2nd row once, every 4th row 14 (15, 18) times—72 (78, 84) sts. Work even until piece measures 8¾ (9½, 10½)"/22 (24, 26.5)cm from beg. Bind off.

FINISHING

Block pieces to measurements.

Pocket flap

With larger needles and H, pick up and k 14 sts from bound-off sts of pocket. **Row 1 (WS)** *K1, p1; rep from * to end. **Row 2** K the purl and p the knit sts. Rep row 2 for seed st for a total of 17 rows. Dec 1 st each side of next row then every other row once. **Next row (RS)** Work 5 sts, yo, k2tog, work to end. Dec 1 st each side of next 2 rows. Bind off 6 sts.

Pocket lining

With larger needles and H, pick up and k 12 sts from cast-on sts of pocket opening. Work in St st for 2"/5cm. Bind off. Sew lining in place. Sew on button under buttonhole on flap. Sew shoulder seams.

With smaller needles and D, pick up and k 91 (95, 99) sts evenly around neck edge. Work in St st for 6 rnds. Bind off. Place markers at 5½ (6, 6½)"/14 (15, 16.5)cm down from shoulders. Sew sleeves to armholes between markers. Sew side and sleeve seams.

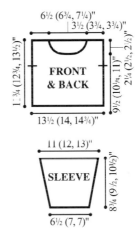

6½ (6¾, 7¼)"
3½ (3¾, 3¾)"
1¾ (12¾, 13½)"
FRONT & BACK
9½ (10¾, 11)"
2¼ (2½, 2½)"
13½ (14, 14¾)"

11 (12, 13)"
SLEEVE
8¾ (9½, 10½)"
6½ (7, 7)"

Color Key

- Blue (A)
- Teal (B)
- Lt blue (C)
- Lt green (D)
- Dk green (E)
- Ecru (F)
- Black (G)
- Beige (H)
- Red (I)

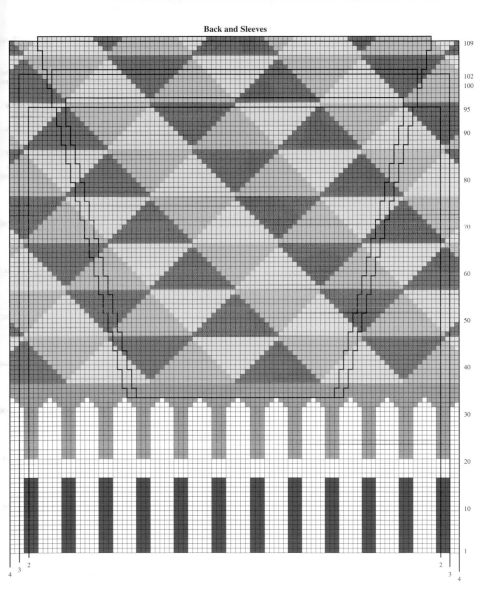

RESOURCES

US RESOURCES

Write to the yarn companies listed below for purchasing and mail-order information.

BAABAJOES WOOL CO.
PO Box 260604
Lakewood, CO 80226

BERROCO, INC.
PO Box 367
Uxbridge, MA 01569

BROWN SPEEP CO.
100662 County Road 16
Mitchell, NE 69357

CLASSIC ELITE YARNS
300 Jackson Street
Lowell, MA 01852

DALE OF NORWAY, INC.
N16 W23390 Stoneridge Dr.
Suite A
Waukesha, WI 53188

DESIGN SOURCE
P O Box 770
Medford, MA 02155

GGH
distributed by
Muench Yarns

JCA
35 Scales Lane
Townsend, MA 01469

KOIGU WOOL DESIGNS
R R #1
Williamsford, ON N0H 2V0
Canada

LANE BORGOSESIA
PO Box 217
Colorado Springs, CO 80903

MANOS DEL URUGUAY
distributed by
Design Source

MISSON FALLS
distributed by
Unique Kolours

MUENCH YARNS
285 Bel Marin Keys Blvd.
Unit J
Novato, CA 94949-5724

NATURALLY
distributed
S. R. Kertzer, Ltd.

PATONS®
PO Box 40
Listowel, ON
N4W 3H3
Canada

PLYMOUTH YARN
PO Box 28
Bristol, PA 19007

REYNOLDS
distributed by
JCA

ROWAN YARNS
5 Northern Blvd.
Amherst, NH 03031

S. R. KERTZER, LTD.
105A Winges Road
Woodbridge, ON L4L 6C2
Canada

SESIA
distributed by
Lane Borgosesia

SCHOELLER ESSLINGER
distributed by
Skacel Collection, Inc.

SKACEL COLLECTION, INC.
PO Box 88110
Seattle, WA 98138-2110

TAHKI•STACY CHARLES, INC.
8000 Cooper Ave.
Building #1
Glendale, NY 11385

TAHKI YARNS
distributed by
Tahki•Stacy Charles, Inc.

UNIQUE KOLOURS
1428 Oak Lane
Downingtown, PA 19335

WOOL PAK YARNS NZ
distributed by
Baabajoes Wool Co.

CANADIAN RESOURCES

Write to US resources for mail-order availability of yarns not listed.

BERROCO, INC.
distributed by
S. R. Kertzer, Ltd.

CLASSIC ELITE YARNS
distributed by
S. R. Kertzer, Ltd.

DIAMOND YARN
9697 St. Laurent
Montreal, PQ H3L 2N1
and
155 Martin Ross, Unit #3
Toronto, ON M3J 2L9

ESTELLE DESIGNS & SALES, LTD.
Units 65/67
2220 Midland Ave.
Scarborough, ON M1P 3E6

KOIGU WOOL DESIGNS
R R #1
Williamsford, ON N0H 2V0

NATURALLY
distributed by
S. R. Kertzer, Ltd.

PATONS ®
PO Box 40
Listowel, ON N4W 3H3

ROWAN
distributed by
Diamond Yarn

S. R. KERTZER, LTD.
105A Winges Rd.
Woodbridge, ON L4L 6C2

SCHOELLER ESSLINGER
distributed by
Diamond Yarn

UK RESOURCES

Not all yarns used in this book are available in the UK. For yarns not available, make a comparable substitute or contact the US manufacturer for purchasing and mail-order information.

ROWAN YARNS
Green Lane Mill
Holmfirth
West Yorks HD7 1RW
Tel: 01484-681881

SILKSTONE
12 Market Place
Cockermouth
Cumbria, CA13 9NQ
Tel: 01900-821052

THOMAS RAMSDEN GROUP
Netherfield Road
Guiseley
West Yorks LS20 9PD
Tel: 01943-872264

VOGUE KNITTING TODDLER KNITS

Editor-in-Chief
TRISHA MALCOLM

Executive Editor
CARLA S. SCOTT

Art Director
CHRISTINE LIPERT

Managing Editor
SUZIE ELIOTT

Instruction Writer
MARI LYNN PATRICK

Technical Illustration Editor/
Page Layout
CHI LING MOY

Instructions Editor
KAREN GREENWALD

Schematics
CHARLOTTE PARRY

Knitting Editor
JEAN GUIRGUIS

Yarn Editor
VERONICA MANNO

Copy Editor
BETTY CHRISTIANSEN

Photography
BRIAN KRAUS, NYC
BOBB CONNORS
Photographed at Butterick Studios

Stylist
MELISSA MARTIN

Production Managers
LILLIAN ESPOSITO
DAVID JOINNIDES

President, Soho Publishing Company
ART JOINNIDES